The LEARNING PRINCIPAL

Becoming a Learning Leader

Kay Psencik,
Frederick Brown, and
Stephanie Hirsh

THE PROFESSIONAL LEARNING ASSOCIATION

Learning Forward
504 S. Locust St.
Oxford, OH 45056
800-727-7288
Fax: 513-523-0638
Email: office@learningforward.org
www.learningforward.org

The Learning Principal: Becoming a Learning Leader
Kay Psencik, Frederick Brown, and Stephanie Hirsh

Editors: Tracy Crow, Joyce Pollard
Designer: Jane Thurmond

Cover image Getty Images; p. 8 Ryan Caron King/Connecticut Public Radio; p.19 courtesy of Fort Wayne Community Schools; p. 24 courtesy of R. Harris; p. 35 courtesy of L. Amstutz-Martin; p. 52 courtesy of D. Martin; p. 62 courtesy of C. Kennedy; p. 73 courtesy of S. Montez; p. 85 courtesy of L. Ceballos; p. 112 courtesy of D. Anthony.

© Learning Forward, 2021.

All rights reserved. Reproduction in whole or part without written permission is prohibited. Unless indicated otherwise, buyers of this book have permission to make up to 30 copies of handouts if they are to be used for instructional purposes as long as this book and Learning Forward are properly cited.

Requests for permission to reprint or copy portions of this book for other purposes must be submitted to Christy Colclasure by fax (513-523-0638) or email (christy.colclasure@learningforward.org). All requests must specify the number of copies that will be made and how the material will be used. Please allow two weeks for a response.

Printed in the United States of America.
Item: B622
ISBN: 978-1-936630-11-0

Contents

Online tools .... **iv**

Acknowledgments .... **v**

Foreword .... **ix**

Introduction .... **xi**

Chapter 1   Prioritizing learning **1**

Chapter 2   Focusing on curriculum **15**

Chapter 3   Managing change **31**

Chapter 4   Designing learning **49**

Chapter 5   Maximizing resources **67**

Chapter 6   Leveraging feedback and coaching **81**

Chapter 7   Applying high standards to principal learning **93**

Chapter 8   Partnering with central offices to support principals **109**

About the authors **124**

About the contributors **126**

www.learningforward.org   The LEARNING PRINCIPAL   **iii**

Online tools

Chapter 1 Prioritizing learning
Tool 1.1 Running a daily self-check
Tool 1.2 Forming an equity mindset for learning
Tool 1.3 Supporting learning teams
Tool 1.4 Listening to students

Chapter 2 Focusing on curriculum
Tool 2.1 Inventorying the curriculum
Tool 2.2 Conducting a curriculum walkthrough
Tool 2.3 Leveraging the curriculum work of learning communities
Tool 2.4 Monitoring the learning cycle

Chapter 3 Managing change
Tool 3.1 Framing a problem of practice
Tool 3.2 Developing a theory of change
Tool 3.3 Writing a logic model
Tool 3.4 Using the Concerns-based Adoption Model and Stages of Concern
Tool 3.5 Establishing and celebrating early wins

Chapter 4 Designing learning
Tool 4.1 Selecting a learning design
Tool 4.2 Designing a learning agenda
Tool 4.3 Advancing equity
Tool 4.4 Using staff agreements and meeting norms
Tool 4.5 Honoring voice and choice

Chapter 5 Maximizing resources
Tool 5.1 Inventorying learning resources and maximizing their use
Tool 5.2 Leveraging internal expertise
Tool 5.3 Finding time for professional learning

Chapter 6 Leveraging feedback and coaching
Tool 6.1 Developing coaching skills and understanding stances
Tool 6.2 Leveraging feedback
Tool 6.3 Practicing committed listening
Tool 6.4 Capturing five insights to wisdom

Chapter 7 Applying high standards to principal learning
Tool 7.1 Conducting a self-assessment of leadership practices
Tool 7.2 Assessing quality of professional learning
Tool 7.3 Mapping standards and building coherence

Chapter 8 Partnering with central offices to support principals
Tool 8.1 Choosing the right partner
Tool 8.2 Clarifying the district-university partnership
Tool 8.3 Using problems of practice to guide improvement
Tool 8.4 Identifying the potential to lead

To access the web page that links to the tools, go to **www.learningforward.org/publications/learning-principal-tools**
Use the password **Leaders!Learn**

Acknowledgments

For more than a decade, Learning Forward has supported continuous learning in schools with its evidence- and practice-oriented resources. Books in the "Becoming a Learning…" series include *Becoming a Learning School, Becoming a Learning System,* and *Becoming a Learning Team: A Guide to a Teacher-led Cycle of Continuous Improvement,* and now *The Learning Principal: Becoming a Learning Leader.*

Evidence has shown that no school-based factor is more important for successful student learning than the individual teacher. And research by Kenneth Leithwood and colleagues (2004) speaks to the principal as "**second only to classroom instruction** among all school-related factors that contribute to what students learn at school" (p. 5).

Conditions of teaching and learning in schools today heighten the need for principals to adopt a learning and improvement mindset. Dramatic changes are required to address inequities that exist in schools, and principals are best positioned to champion new and better policies, practices, and procedures. Once again, Leithwood and colleagues (2004) remind us that "…there are **virtually no documented instances of troubled schools being turned around without intervention by a powerful leader**. Many other factors may contribute to such turnarounds, but leadership is the catalyst" (p. 5).

Our experiences have affirmed this finding again and again.

We believe that if appropriately applied, the ideas and strategies promoted in *The Learning Principal* will contribute to principals' increasing their

impact on student learning by acting as what Paul Manna (2015) refers to as a "multiplier of learning." When applying guidance from the text, principals will, we expect, experience and model high-quality professional learning — professional learning that is long term, sustained, and standards driven; grounded in a cycle of continuous improvement; and capable of advancing school cultures free of racism and bigotry.

Among we three co-authors, this book represents decades of hands-on experiences working with principals.

. . .

First, from Fred Brown:

My principalship gave me a huge appreciation of the complexity of the work of the building leader. Many years ago, when I first aspired to be a building leader, I thought I had a solid sense of what the job entailed. After all, I had watched my own principal do it in a way that seemed extremely manageable. Little did I know about all the factors contributing to her "effortless" success. Once I sat in the principal's seat, I quickly realized just how complex the role can be. Serving as the leader of learning for the students and the adults was a challenge that I was ready to embrace, yet I needed support to be successful.

Since leaving my principalship, I've had the opportunity to support aspiring and practicing principals at the district level in Chicago and nationally through my work as a senior program officer at The Wallace Foundation. In both of those roles I developed

ACKNOWLEDGMENTS

a deep appreciation of research- and evidence-based strategies for building leaders. Leaders don't have to feel like they are constantly reinventing the wheel. As a field, we've learned so much about what good leaders do and the systems of support that are needed to ensure their success.

• • •

From Kay Psencik:

As supervisor for principals in Austin and Temple Independent School Districts (ISDs), I saw first-hand the critical role that principals played in the success of teachers and students. I made it a priority to develop skills essential to engage principals in long-term sustained professional learning. We learned about the power of the principal taking the lead in focusing professional learning communities in the school on curriculum work, on building a collaborative culture, and on connecting all their work to student data.

Through my 11 years as the facilitator for the Twin Tiers Principals Coalition for Learning, serving more than 150 principals in the Twin Tiers Region of upstate New York, we intentionally built learning communities of principals who focused on student performance data and curriculum analysis in support of the work of their teachers' learning communities. We are so grateful to Katherine Funk, executive director of the Twin Tiers Coalition for Learning and The Corning Foundation for supporting that effort for 11 years.

• • •

From Stephanie Hirsh:

My contributions were informed by decades of listening to and learning from principals as a director of professional development, facilitator for the Learning Forward Academy, which graduated hundreds of principals in its 20+ years of operation, and more. Books and research focused on the role of principal learning always caught my attention.

In particular, The Wallace Foundation Principal Pipeline and Principal Supervisor initiatives have been instrumental in shaping our thinking. The work that The Wallace Foundation has done in unpacking the linkages among leadership standards, preservice experiences for principals, hiring and placement procedures, ongoing support and evaluation of leaders, and the particular importance of the role of the principal supervisor, will shape leadership systems in schools and districts for many years to come.

Through all of these efforts, we refined our view of the importance of professional learning for principals. We also learned that district support for principal professional learning and effective district-level supervision was essential if principal learning were to affect improved practice and school outcomes. We applied that learning to the more recent design and execution of the Galveston County Learning Leaders Community, funded by Houston Endowment. Superintendents and deputy superintendents in Galveston County, Dr. Leigh Wall, Santa Fe ISD; Dr. Greg Smith, Clear Creek ISD; Dr. Steve Ebell, Clear Creek ISD; Dr. Kelli Moulton, Galveston ISD; Thad Locklear, Friendswood ISD; and Diane Myers, Friendswood ISD, unequivocally included principals in their learning community and focused their attention on their needs.

Learning Leaders for Learning Schools, a collaborative between Learning Forward and the Arizona Department of Education, was funded by the American Express Principals Path to Leadership grant program. The program included seminars, small communities of practice, and personalized coaching. A multimedia field guide co-developed with participants was a product and informed this text.

Equally important to our experiences were the insights and experiences offered by Jim Knight, senior partner of the Instructional Coaching Group and

ACKNOWLEDGMENTS

the outstanding principals and former school leaders showcased throughout this book.

We are grateful to our colleague Jim Knight who shared his observations in the Foreword. Jim has advanced the study of school leaders and coaches, and we are honored to have his voice in this book.

We also are fortunate to have had opportunities to work with, champion, and learn from the former and current school leaders who offer their experience and insights. Their contributions enrich the book by making it more accessible, authentic, and meaningful for readers. (See list of Contributors to *The Learning Principal*.)

• • •

Finally, we are indebted to our production team, beginning with Learning Forward Chief Strategy Officer and editor extraordinaire, Tracy Crow who stuck with us through the more than three years it took to finalize this text. Editor Joyce Pollard also refined the text and worked with the school leader contributors to develop their profiles. Graphics designer Jane Thurmond designed the cover, layout of the book, and coordinated production.

The three of us acknowledge that the work we do could not be accomplished without the loving support of our families. Thanks to their cheerleading, foregoing time with us, and taking the lead on family commitments, we have been able to concentrate on the challenging task of writing. We love them and thank them for partnering with us in another endeavor.

Contributors to *The Learning Principal*

Lindsay Amstutz-Martin
Principal, Fairfield Elementary School
Fort Wayne Community Schools
Fort Wayne, Indiana

J.R. Ankenbruck
Principal, Mabel K. Holland Elementary School
Fort Wayne Community Schools
Fort Wayne, Indiana

Douglas W. Anthony
Chief Consultant, Anthony Consulting Group
Former Associate Superintendent
Prince George's County Public Schools
Upper Marlboro, Maryland

Leslie Ceballos
Assistant Principal, Dr. E.T. Boon Elementary School
Allen ISD
Allen, Texas

Leilani Esmond
Director, Department of Staff Development
Gwinnett County Public Schools
Gwinnett County, Georgia

Rachel Harris
Principal, Santa Fe High School
Santa Fe ISD
Santa Fe, Texas

Carrie Kennedy
Principal, Fred H. Croninger Elementary School
Fort Wayne Community Schools
Fort Wayne, Indiana

ACKNOWLEDGMENTS

Destini Martin
Principal, William F. Barnett Elementary School
Santa Fe ISD
Santa Fe, Texas

Stephanie Montez
Principal, Adams Elementary School
Mesa Public Schools
Mesa, Arizona

Azra Redzic
Elementary Humanities Supervisor
Bristol Public Schools
Former Principal, Maria Sanchez Elementary School
Bristol, Connecticut

Christel Swinehart-Arbogast
Principal, Emerson Elementary School
Mesa Public Schools
Mesa, Arizona

Foreword

For the past 28 years, I've been associated with the Center for Research on Learning at the University of Kansas. At first I studied learning strategies, the metacognitive processes that we could teach students so they would become better learners. Then I studied learning organizations, groups of people who work together in ways that lead to a higher collective IQ than the IQ of any individual. I've even written about learning strategies for learning organizations.

Throughout my nearly three decades of work, I've always been vividly aware of the importance of learning. I often say, in fact, that if you made a list of the three to five most important elements of a fulfilling life, learning would have to be on your list. A life where people are denied the opportunity to learn, or where people simply choose to stop learning, is an impoverished life. As Peter Senge has written in one of my favorite quotations from *The Fifth Discipline* (1990), all of us share a deep hunger for learning:

> Real learning gets to the heart of what it means to be human. Through learning we reperceive the world and our relationship to it. Through learning we extend our capacity to create, to be part of the generative process of life. There is within each of us a deep hunger for this type of learning. (p. 14)

Senge's words have always resonated deeply for me, but never more than now. As I write this, the United States is beset by three profoundly unsettling realities. First, we are at the mercy of COVID-19, a virus that is upsetting the experiences of everyone living in the United States. All of us are striving to make impossible predictions about our careers and our loved ones, and that uncertainty has most of us recalling normal times and wondering if we'll ever see them again.

Second, the country, let us hope, is finally awakening to the horrible consequences of over 400 years of systemic racism and oppressive action against people of color. Inspired by others and fired by anger, many Americans have taken to the streets to say "Enough is enough," and it is time for change. As a result, many leaders in schools and elsewhere have recognized that they must change how they see their world and how they act. Increasingly, they share an acceptance of the most important change — that ALL students receive the excellent education they deserve so they can realize the potential they carry.

Finally, meaningful political discourse has been nearly impossible given an extremely divisive political climate. This polarization has been amplifying dissonance even as we try to wake up to racism and avoid the virus. People are frightened about their health, angry about racism, and longing to talk about any of that with people who matter to them. In the midst of all of this turmoil, somehow, principals must create safe settings for learning without knowing whether that learning will occur in their schools or remotely.

If they are going to succeed, principals need to be learners, and especially what the authors refer to as "lead learners." To embody this mindset, as you will see in the pages of *The Learning Principal*, leaders need

FOREWORD

to be intentional about leading learning. Often, as I have learned from Kay Psencik, Frederick Brown, and Stephanie Hirsh, "leading learning" means that principals must accept the tension of paradox. Principals must set high expectations and honor the autonomy and professionalism of teachers. They must directly confront implicit bias and be excellent, responsive, learning listeners. Principals must build coherence with a change plan and accept the adaptive nature of change.

Leading a school has always been incredibly challenging and incredibly important. As the authors state here, no meaningful school improvement is possible without an effective leader. And never has the job of being a principal been more challenging. Fortunately, this book is packed with tools that will help all principals reflect on learning in their individual lives and lead learning in their schools. For example, there are tools that principals can use to create a plan for change and others they can use to reflect on their own readiness for change. Building on much that Learning Forward has said about learning and leading, this book is packed with material that will help any leader make a greater impact.

I'm reminded nowadays of my one other favorite quotation about learning from Eric Hoffer, the so-called longshoreman philosopher. Hoffer writes: "In times of change, learners inherit the earth while the learned find themselves beautifully equipped for a world that no longer exists." I first heard this famous quotation in 1989, but it seems more relevant today than ever before. The principals who guide their schools through these days will have to be learners; fortunately for them, they have this book to help them with that absolutely essential task.

— Jim Knight
Senior Partner
Instructional Coaching Group
Lawrence, Kansas

Introduction

Learning is the foundation for high-performing schools where all staff and students achieve and perform at high levels. Driven by their deep intention to make a substantive difference for each and every student, principals prioritize learning for themselves. As the chief learner in a school, principals constantly strive to identify and take actions that advance equity and excellence for all.

This learning orientation is more important than ever. As of this writing, school leaders everywhere are faced with the unexpected challenge of schooling during a global pandemic. The initial onset of COVID-19 in the spring of 2020 introduced one set of challenges to principals, who worked tirelessly to ensure that students in their communities were fed and safe before turning to the question of how best to continue and sustain meaningful learning experiences given widespread inequalities in access to technology tools, Internet, and spaces and support for remote learning. Principals and teachers focused their immediate learning efforts on building their capacity to teach effectively online and to make sense of adapting instructional materials to a virtual context.

As the pandemic continued, the challenges proliferated, with school and system leaders creating plans for multiple schooling configurations and an uncertain year ahead. A focus on keeping all students and staffs safe required principals to develop an entirely new set of knowledge and skills related to public health and advocacy for their communities in an unprecedented situation. Working in partnership with district leaders, principals seek to balance the many needs their students, families, and communities face and to create schooling configurations that address those needs.

At the same time, long-standing inequities in schools, not least the systemic racism built into so many aspects of education, have never been more apparent or explicit. The yawning gaps between what students of color and white students experienced during the early months of remote teaching were the first alarm bell related to equity to ring in the spring of 2020.

Protests in the U.S. against police brutality following the killing of George Floyd in Minneapolis heightened the awareness of and demand to confront ongoing systemic racism through all facets of society. Educators at every level are recognizing the urgent need to address racist and inequitable structures, policies, and practices so that every student they serve has access to a promising future.

As a result, the need for great principals is more critical than ever. Great principals are first and foremost committed to success for each and every student. They know that key to that success is the quality of teaching and learning experienced in classrooms every day. While the particulars of this moment in 2020 will shift over time, the enduring inequities that have been so starkly exposed must remain a focus for educator conversations until all students are given opportunities

INTRODUCTION

to attend great schools staffed by excellent teachers and led by great principals.

This requires that both teachers and students be granted the guidance, support, and resources essential to learning and performing at high levels each day. The school leaders who embrace their roles as learning principal serve as the guiding lights for the difficult changes required in each school context.

- A learning principal commits to continuous improvement as the foundation for ensuring equity and excellence.
- A learning principal shares responsibility for decision making and recognizes that the best decisions are informed by study, collaboration, and consideration of multiple perspectives and voices.
- A learning principal understands adult learning research and theories and applies those meticulously in designing professional learning for educators.
- A learning principal focuses on the instructional core, recognizing that the relationship between the teacher, the student including their context and race, and the curriculum are key to students' meeting and exceeding expectations.
- A learning principal prioritizes building capacity of self and all staff in cultural competence and differentiation.
- A learning principal embraces each role and responsibility including supervisor, coach, learning designer, facilitator, and advocate to bring out the very best in others.

Learning Forward has invested the last decade in a number of initiatives to support principals. As a grantee of The Wallace Foundation, Houston Endowment, and American Express, Learning Forward staff and consultants have been given access to researchers, technical assistance providers, and thought leaders who think and lead in new ways. Long-term technical assistance contracts in Corning, New York; Fort Wayne, Indiana; Santa Fe, Texas; and others have provided incredible learning laboratories for testing emerging research and documenting its impact. These experiences, as well as Learning Forward's tools and resources that translate research into practice, inform the ideas discussed in this book.

The precursors to *The Learning Principal* include *The Learning Educator* (Killion and Hirsh), *Becoming a Learning Team* (Hirsh and Crow), *Becoming a Learning School* (Killion and Roy), and *Becoming a Learning System* (Brown, Psencik, and Hirsh). This book offers a point of view on how a principal applies a learning lens to each key responsibility. Through that learning lens the principal is able to find new ways to strengthen impact and the potential of the entire faculty. The final chapter examines what school systems do to ensure all principals get the support they need to become learning principals.

The primary audience for this book is principals. Aspiring principals, however, may read it to determine the degree to which their beliefs and practices align with the roles and responsibilities of learning principals. They may look for opportunities in their current roles to take a learning stance toward their work every day. Principal supervisors and other district officials may read the book to look for ways to shift policies and practices that support hiring of learning principals. They may also pay attention to the key practices of principal supervisors who have responsibility for guiding and supporting learning principals.

The Learning Principal offers a vision, expectations, roles, and responsibilities that define a high-performing school leader. With each new challenge that principals face, an intentional orientation to learning will ensure they are prepared to seek knowledge and identify solutions that place students' equitable outcomes at the fore.

INTRODUCTION

Readers will find these elements in each chapter:

Where are we now?	These statements allow readers to think about their school and the key concepts addressed in the chapter. The statements begin with a generic "The principal," but are intended for the principal as reader to replace "The principal…" with "I…" and for others to consider the role generally, a single principal for study, or the many principals one supervises.
Narrative	The narrative offers assumptions and foundational knowledge on the subject including overarching ideas, key research findings, and field-based exemplars to promote deeper understanding, thoughtful action, and ongoing reflection.
Next actions	This section offers three to five specific actions that principals may take to address the key ideas advanced in the chapter. Explanations are included and in many cases readers are directed to accompanying tools to make the next steps more accessible.
Reflections	The questions are offered to encourage readers to examine their commitment to becoming a learning principal and consider subsequent actions they may need to take. By recording and reviewing responses, principals can examine their thinking, analyze progress, redirect actions, and celebrate progress.
Tools index	The tools index directs readers to accompanying online resources referenced in the chapter that will help initiate recommendations in the chapter.
References	Each chapter offers a list of references included in the text.

www.learningforward.org

The LEARNING PRINCIPAL **xiii**

CHAPTER 1

Prioritizing learning

Where are we now?

The principal values her own learning and the learning of others in the school.

STRONGLY AGREE — AGREE — NO OPINION — DISAGREE — STRONGLY DISAGREE

The principal engages in professional learning with staff to promote collective responsibility for the learning of all.

STRONGLY AGREE — AGREE — NO OPINION — DISAGREE — STRONGLY DISAGREE

Strong levels of trust exist between the principal and staff as well as between the principal and students.

STRONGLY AGREE — AGREE — NO OPINION — DISAGREE — STRONGLY DISAGREE

The principal visibly makes clear the high expectations held for staff and students.

STRONGLY AGREE — AGREE — NO OPINION — DISAGREE — STRONGLY DISAGREE

The principal has established a culture where innovation and risk-taking are essential.

STRONGLY AGREE — AGREE — NO OPINION — DISAGREE — STRONGLY DISAGREE

CHAPTER 1

When a learning principal instills a growth mindset in adults and students, leadership matters. A leader who is a lifelong learner sets the stage for professional learning and classroom improvement and makes continual refinement visible in every aspect of her practice. Learning principals approach every situation as learners; they constantly reflect on their practice, network, and learn from others. By taking a learning mindset, learning principals create opportunities for continuous improvement that directly affects staff and student cultures.

Azra Redzic
Elementary Humanities Supervisor
Bristol Public Schools
Former Principal, Maria Sanchez Elementary School
Bristol, Connecticut

Overview

Highly effective principals relentlessly pursue equity and excellence. To that end, one of their priorities is professional learning that leads to high-quality teaching and learning for every student every day. They communicate the school's mission and moral purpose throughout all actions. With a commitment to equity at the core, principals take every action necessary to ensure teachers have support, resources, and expertise to not only meet the immediate needs of students, but to provide them access to a future with limitless possibilities. Jason Grissom's (2011) analyses showed that

> The effectiveness of the school principal is found to be an especially important component of teacher working conditions; average teacher ratings of principal effectiveness are strong predictors of teacher job satisfaction and one-year turnover probability in the average school. Moreover, these correlations are even stronger in schools with large numbers of disadvantaged students that traditionally have faced greater staffing challenges. (p. 2574)

To put every educator's continuous improvement at the fore, principals demonstrate that they are learning principals. They value their own learning and lead by example to engage in learning with staff and other principals. A learning principal regularly reflects on her work and its impact on students and staff to determine where she needs to change her practice. She sets new goals for herself and engages in the practice of learning new skills or behaviors.

Learning principals believe that when adults are continuously learning, students will succeed. Their unshakable commitment is based on building collective responsibility for the success of **all** students. Learning principals also create the conditions and provide the support necessary for all staff members as well as members of the broader school community to engage in cycles of learning and improvement. Learning principals display attitudes of respect, joy, and optimism for the potential within each educator and student. Their attitudes permeate the school and in many cases, principals, staff, and students produce results that once may have been viewed as unattainable.

Leithwood, Louis, Anderson, and Wahlstrom (2004) conclude that principals are "second only to classroom instruction among all school-related factors that contribute to what students learn at school" (p. 5). Leithwood and his colleagues' study firmly establishes that principals make an impact on student outcomes. But what do they **do** that matters? As this book explores in depth, effective principals focus intentionally on learning for all. Among their intentions, learning principals set high expectations and challenging learning goals for students and staff; they expect all educators in their schools to learn together every day in pursuit of individual, team, school, and district learning goals; and they build cultures of trust for such ongoing learning and risk-taking to happen as teachers and staff work collectively to help every student learn and meet expectations.

Expectations drive results

Learning principals are recognized for the high expectations they hold for students and staff. High expectations are recognizable through the mission and goals that drive the learning agenda. Hirsh and Killion (2007) write that ambitious goals lead to powerful actions and remarkable results. They contend that bold goals offer motivation and pressure to succeed. Jim Collins and Jerry Porras (1994) coined the expression Big Hairy Audacious Goals (BHAGs) to describe how visionary organizations drive boldly toward their aspirations based on their core values. Such goals don't just exist in parallel to ideology; they are manifestations of it. They are extensions of who educators are and what matters to them (p. 170). In learning schools, principals enlist the entire community including all school staff, families, and community partners in the development of audacious goals. Learning principals know that professional learning takes on new meaning when educators commit seriously to high expectations and achieving powerful goals.

As the counterpart to holding high expectations, learning principals create a culture of support and caring. They recognize the hard work — and ongoing support — required to achieve high expectations. They establish an environment in which staff and students know each other well and treat each other with respect. Hard work can be stressful so principals focus significant energy in building caring relationships with and among staff. They establish a blame-free zone of learning. Learning principals believe that when people are committed and connected to everyone in the school, they will invest the time necessary to achieve ambitious goals. Principals know that teachers being fully engaged with their learning community, their students, and their administrators inspires them to do their best work.

The principal's expectation for caring and respectful relationships extends to interactions with families and community members. Learning principals create an environment in which families and community are treated as essential partners in the education of their students. Parents feel welcome and know they have a voice in their child's education. Learning principals encourage parents who want to and can be at school to serve as mentors for students or resources in the classroom. When principals create a culture of inclusion, learning, and joy, everyone in the school thrives. Principals also invite partners from the broader school

CHAPTER 1

community to extend the culture and ensure resources and support not otherwise available to teachers.

Principals accompany their high expectations with a commitment to build strong relationships with students, knowing each student's progress and challenges. Learning principals are constantly analyzing data about student progress and engaging in meaningful conversations with staff, families, and students about how students are doing. They chart progress student by student, teacher by teacher, and skill by skill over time. They are not just focused on numbers; they examine artifacts of student work and they talk to students. As they consider teachers' learning needs and those connections with student learning, effective principals observe adult practices and the impact that specific teaching approaches have on student behaviors, attitudes, and outcomes. They choose protocols for hosting thoughtful data conversations. Such protocols help guide learning teams through conversations about relationships, including possible causal factors, next actions to take with students, and the essential learning that adults need to discover effective ways to meet student needs.

Learning principals recognize that it is irresponsible to present compelling "stretch" goals without also providing the support needed to achieve them. They work to ensure all staff feel valued and empowered to achieve the school's mission and fulfill its moral purpose. By modeling respectful language, attitudes, and actions and a relentless focus on outcomes, they send a message that both high expectations and strong relationships are critical to success.

Every educator learns every day

Fundamental to achieving equity and excellence is a commitment to continuous learning. Learning principals lead learning schools. Learning schools are distinguished by the priority they place on learning for students and staff members alike. Learning schools are places where all parents have confidence in the children's teachers because they know teachers share collective responsibility for the success of all students in a grade level, in a particular course, and across the school from year to year. Learning principals ensure that the conditions and support are in place so that teachers have what is necessary to advance their knowledge, understanding, and practice.

The principal's attitude toward professional learning and her understanding of the Standards for Professional Learning and the cycle of continuous improvement determine the school's approach to professional learning. The principal does not lead all instructional learning but works to ensure that intense instructional focus and continuous learning are central. Highly effective principals build a culture for learning, tap others to co-lead, and serve as learning leaders for all. Learning principals recognize when it is time to lead and when it is time to collaborate and learn.

Learning principals believe the core work of the learning teams or communities is anchored in high-quality instructional materials. William Schmidt and Nathan Burroughs (2013) report,

> As it stands now, students' chances to learn challenging content depend on whether they are lucky enough to attend a school that provides it. In effect, a defense of localism in response to questions about content amounts to a defense of inequality in opportunity to learn. (p. 5)

TNTP (2018) reports that low-income students are less likely than high-income students to have access to high-quality content and grade-appropriate lessons. Learning principals guided by principles of equity and excellence ensure that all classrooms have high-quality materials to support effective instruction.

Access to high-quality instructional materials is only part of the essential equation for achieving equity and excellence. Studying and adapting high-quality instructional materials is the other half. This work has among the greatest potential to transform all students' learning experiences. Learning principals ensure that educators' learning agendas are grounded in the curriculum and that teachers use learning cycles to identify student challenges and their greatest needs in understanding, implementing, and supplementing or adapting materials and strategies to ensure the success of all students. When teachers invest ongoing dedicated time to study materials, they set the foundation for transferring their learning into powerful lessons that can be differentiated and personalized to address individual student needs. High-quality lessons that motivate, engage, and challenge students enable them to achieve the success learning educators desire for them (Hirsh, 2018). Principals secure substantial time during the work day for learning teams to learn together and offer specialized training and support for the learning team facilitator.

Learning principals maximize the talent in their school and individual learning teams and support leadership development among educators at every level. Paul Manna (2015) calls such principals "multipliers":

> Principals who are strong, effective, responsive leaders help to inspire and enhance the abilities of their teachers and other school staff to do excellent work. Such principals also tend to retain great teachers and create opportunities for them to take on new leadership roles. In short, principals, through their actions, can be powerful multipliers of effective teaching and leadership practices in schools. (p. 7)

Learning principals attract and hire teachers who view it as a professional obligation to continue to learn.

Learning principals also serve as lead learners. The learning principal is constantly asking: "How can I get smarter to help this team in a better way?" Learning principals speak up and show everyone how to make sure that "At our school, everyone's job is to learn."

Trust builds courage

Trust is a key element if learning is to result in substantive change. Successful trust builders demonstrate certain attributes and take deliberate actions. Principals build trust when they are open and vulnerable while holding expectations high. Principals who are trustworthy are viewed as honest, fair, and consistent in their transactions. They keep their promises and admit when they made mistakes. Trusted principals lead communities to see schools as a laboratory for learning for both students and staff. Through this work, people take ownership for their own learning, the learning of their peers, and the learning of all students. They feel empowered to assume and share leadership responsibilities and take necessary actions. Trust becomes the connective tissue in which high expectations, purposeful teaching and learning, and community flourish.

This culture of trust nurtures the courage to embrace new ideas and experimentation. Principals continuously create conditions that result in teams exploring new research, innovations, and strategies. Staff members feel empowered to take risks and learning from failure. Sharing instructional practices, modeling, co-teaching, observing each other, and asking for help from peers and the principal are celebrated and encouraged as opportunities to learn. People are sincere about their own learning, their commitment to their students, and the confidence that they can do whatever it takes to ensure the success of all their students. This innovative environment is nurtured through high levels of trust in the organization.

CHAPTER 1

Stephen M. R. Covey (2008) writes that effective leaders remember that their thoughts, attitudes, and actions are self-fulfilling proficiencies. When they lead with positive self-expectancy, confidence, optimism, and just plain faith, they can expect wins and can lead through the challenges. An effective football coach once told us, "When you feel like you have hit the wall and you do not see your way out, when you are exhausted and going into survival mode, lift up your head, lift your energy, and pick up the pace. It's your choice!" The principal has the responsibility to carry through and finish strong. When staff members view the principal as a finisher — someone of character with high expectations of them — they are confident that the principal can be trusted to work with them through any challenges to create positive teaching and learning conditions for all students and staff.

Taking action

Principals who are intentional about making learning the priority for their schools are careful in how they choose to spend their time each day. They choose actions and words that demonstrate their commitment to learning for all. The following actions are helpful to principals seeking to strengthen and amplify this responsibility.

1. Run a self-check every morning

Given the importance of the learning principal's commitment to learning, high expectations, and a thriving culture, how she shows up each day sets the tone for the school. Learning principals ask, "What attitude am I bringing with me to school today? What impact will that attitude have on the work of others and the success of students?" Checking ourselves with a whole-body and mindset scan makes a difference.

Principals have control over the attitude they bring to school every day and they are under constant observation. What principals do, how they do it, and what they say all matter in terms of what others do and say.

Co-author Psencik recalled a friend's observations in doctors' waiting rooms: "When the doctor is not in the office, things run fine — everyone is very professional, but there is a low energy level among the staff. When the doctor walks in the front door, energy is noticeably higher. People are laughing, they begin moving just a little faster, there is a lift in their voices as they joke with each other. It is amazing what a difference one person can make in the attitudes and energies of those around them!" Principals have the same impact. When principals show up exhibiting no energy, feeling tired, holding a negative attitude about themselves and the world in which they live, they can expect to see similar behaviors from others.

Check yourself. Ask, "What does my attitude, body, and language today model for others? What are my expectations of myself today? How will my energy level show that? What is the mood I want to project for others? If I am in a mood of anger or frustration, how will others treat each other and the students we serve? If I am in a mood of optimism and hope, will it be strong enough to be infectious? How can I turn myself around to best serve others?"

Robert Kegan and Lisa Lahey (2001) remind us that without this self-assessment, it may be nearly impossible for us to bring about the changes we desire.

If we say, "I haven't the time for all this soul-searching. Let's just jump in, get into action, and we'll work out the problems as we come upon them," it's easy to predict that we will end up puzzled as to why such good intentions led to such disappointing results. (p. 63)

PRIORITIZING LEARNING

Living by the PEER Code: Learning with peers and students

Learning principals focus intensely on student learning. To sharpen that focus, they create a learning culture based on a continuous improvement process, one each for students and staff. Like gears, the two cycles mesh with adult learning making a direct impact on what and how students learn. A learning principal provides for strategic design of professional learning to ensure that teachers gain the knowledge and skills they need in their cycle to help students meet learning goals in theirs.

As the former principal of Maria Sanchez Elementary School, I led the development of our school culture and schoolwide expectations. The staff and administration, with consultation from EL Education school designers, crafted a schoolwide code of norms focused on student learning. The norms became the foundation of our culture while our collaborative creation and input allowed us to develop shared commitment to the continuous improvement process. The Sanchez School became known as the PEER Code School. The acronym PEER stands for Perseverance, Enthusiasm, Exploration, and Respect. In every aspect of learning — student and adult — we applied the PEER Code by persevering through challenges; demonstrating enthusiasm in daily lessons, interactions, and operations; exploring ideas; and respecting all stakeholders.

To stay focused on learning, we initiated several structures, including explicit teaching of PEER norms, teacher-led walkthroughs, feedback for improvement, flex intervention/enrichment blocks, grade-level cohorts, student goal-setting and student-led conferences. In morning CREW meetings, staff explicitly taught the PEER Code to students while simultaneously modeling these elements through

P.E.E.R. CODE

Perseverance

- O **I CAN keep trying without giving up.**

- O **I CAN use my strategies and try my best to complete an assigned task.**

Enthusiasm

- O **I CAN have a positive attitude.**

- O **I CAN celebrate and energize myself and others.**

Exploration

- O **I CAN leave my comfort zone and take risks.**

- O **I CAN independently explore and extend my learning.**

- O **I CAN welcome new challenges.**

Respect

- O **I CAN follow the PEER Code at all times and make smart choices even when others are not.**

- O **I CAN treat others the way I want to be treated.**

- O **I CAN respect my school community.**

Maria Sánchez Elementary School   EL Education

CHAPTER 1

Former Principal Azra Redzic championed standards at Sanchez Elementary School.

daily interactions with students and each other. The PEER Code, displayed, referenced, and embedded within the day, was essential to supporting student academics. Teacher-led walkthroughs let teachers visit one another's classrooms while providing job-embedded professional learning and a means for sharing feedback with colleagues in identified focus areas.

As our schoolwide learning culture matured, so did staff collaboration resulting in high levels of adult learning. School staff, for example, strengthened their sense of ownership and responsibility for their own learning; I was able, later, to distribute leadership among staff members to lead improvement efforts. Staff met weekly and created teacher action plans to support the Flex (Intervention/Enrichment) blocks. This block of time was strategically designed to intervene and create enrichments based on identified student strengths and areas of need. Staff teams analyzed formal and informal data to create individualized student and personalized adult learning opportunities. The PEER Code/CREW philosophy, which was so deeply ingrained in the staff, gave rise to a community in which staff embraced all students and taught them outside their own class and grade level. Teacher teams created grade-level cohorts to manage this practice.

Embracing our continuous improvement process, we expanded our learning capacity quickly. And we demonstrated higher achievement than we thought possible. As teachers led students through the process of crafting and reflecting on their own academic goals, they changed the parent-teacher conference structure. Students engaged in goal setting, self-monitoring, and reflection to achieve their goals. They took ownership of their own learning and reported their progress and growth.

For all of us at Maria Sanchez, I'd say we were able to sustain our learning focus because the continuous improvement process addressed student and staff learning needs concurrently. With a schoolwide focus on learning, students and staff can learn collaboratively, take ownership for their learning and progress more quickly, elevate achievement, and ingrain all stakeholders with a commitment to learning.

— *Azra Redzic*

Theirs is a caution to leaders who may have a great desire to foster a more collaborative learning organization. Yet, without a self-check, their leadership and language may actually be communicating an authoritative leadership style. Intentionally performing morning self-checks (see Tool 1.1: Running a Daily Self-Check) is an amazingly powerful process to position a principal for greater success each day.

2. Model commitment to professional learning

Each educator has a personal responsibility to learn aggressively, and principals are no different. Education is evolving rapidly and each individual who impacts student learning has a responsibility to set individual goals for learning along with a course to achieve them. Each educator needs a personal learning agenda grounded in an equity mindset, school goals, and theory of change. Although unique, each learning agenda is focused on developing new skills, competencies, and behaviors to advance an educator's goals (see Tool 1.2: Forming an Equity Mindset for Learning).

The Leadership standard (Learning Forward, 2011) calls on leaders for action:

> As advocates for professional learning, leaders make their own career-long learning visible to others. They participate in professional learning within and beyond their own work environment. Leaders consume information in multiple fields to enhance their leadership practice. Through learning, they clarify their values and beliefs and their influence on others and on the achievement of organizational goals. Their actions model attitudes and behaviors they expect of all educators. (pp. 29–30)

Learning leaders model the learning practices and attitudes they expect of others. They set and share their individual learning goals. They chart their own personal learning journey. They engage with staff members and other principals as well as colleagues beyond the school system to acquire the knowledge and skills they need to achieve their goals. They make public what they are reading and implications of it for their work. They reflect and write about their new learning in order to get clarity and when appropriate share their thoughts with others. They participate in staff learning, including in learning teams and experiences organized strictly for principals. They commit to collaboration and demonstrate their belief that learning with others leads to faster results. Learning principals are committed to identifying and engaging in their own learning communities. They elevate this work and the impact it has on them for their school and community.

3. Be the guardian of learning teams

Create conditions for team success. Start the year with a clearly articulated cycle for each team. Ensure that each learning team understands its roles and responsibilities. Introduce or review the learning cycle you expect all teams to follow and ensure they have necessary resources including data, instructional materials, assessments, and time to do the work. Establish a year-long calendar for the data conversations you set with all teams. Ensure teams have effective facilitators and if necessary enhance them with additional learning or external support.

Attend learning team sessions. Continue to reinforce the importance of a focus on curriculum, instruction, and assessment and elevate examples of how this matters in terms of student success. When you notice other topics such as behavior in the classroom or students' failure to do homework creeping into learning team conversations, gently confront and bring teams back to their essential work.

CHAPTER 1

Even when you feel overbooked and stressed to get everything done in a timely manner, make it a priority to attend learning team sessions. Successful principals make time to participate and engage in conversations about curriculum, assessment, and instruction. Schedule your time in the learning communities and protect it.

Tammy Bock, an associate principal in Friendswood ISD, Friendswood, Texas, was committed to building the capacity of her 7th-grade ELA team in increasing their effectiveness in teaching writing. She had been monitoring the data with them for several years. Student writing scores on the state test were stagnant. Bock believed in her team and knew they could learn their way to success. As they analyzed their student performance data, she observed and was pleased when they agreed that they could do much better. She provided materials and expertise to support their examination of more effective approaches to teaching writing. She provided resources necessary to enable them to observe teachers in a nearby district implementing strategies they were interested in using. She participated in team learning sessions as they refined their vision for excellent writing instruction. She reminded them to follow through with a strong implementation plan. The team put into place strategies for planning together, establishing a classroom environment conducive to writing, observing each other teaching, engaging in feedback and coaching conversations, and making modifications to their work. As they became more proficient at their work, she encouraged them to analyze the impact on their students. They found a significant increase in their students' skills in writing. The outcomes increased their commitment to the work they were undertaking. See Tool 1.2: Supporting Learning Teams to consider other ways to strengthen learning teams.

4. Learn from students

Principals who value their relationships with their students spend time with them. They schedule opportunities for students to share their experiences in school and their attitudes about how things can be better. In addition, principals determine strategies to facilitate students taking responsibility for their own learning and the learning of their peers. Principals focus on learning from students about what principal, faculty, and community actions are helpful and what are barriers to their efficacy and success.

Principals learn from students in various ways. They engage students in both formal and informal listening and learning structures. They host regular focus groups with students or hold lunchtime conversations. They invite students to share what is or is not working for them in terms of classroom assignments, relationships with teachers, and expectations of them. They engage in one-on-one conversations about the rigor and expectations students are experiencing in the classroom. They visit classrooms and ask students about their current work and its application for them.

Kent Ewing, retired Bowie High School principal in Austin ISD, Austin, Texas, made his relationships with students a priority. He put students on his school leadership team. He charged a student group to develop a schedule that would work best for all students. Students were offered different arrival and exit times to meet unique needs and course requirements. The schedule also created opportunities for flexible teacher schedules. Students also determined that some courses could be completed in a month and other courses could be taught by adults in the community over lunch and last a couple of weeks. Students indicated that time in class should not matter as much as their ability to demonstrate competency on the standards. Ewing was intent on listening and he supported changes to respond to what he heard.

There are so many possibilities for prioritizing student voices. Planning a pizza party to talk about how all students are not attending school regularly might result in a conversation about what the school could do differently to support them in coming to school or to better understand the issues students are facing. Principals can schedule home visits throughout the year to check in with students and parents. Principals can host and attend after-school opportunities on activities of interest to students — bowling, camping, computer program design, painting, sewing — anything to create time to be with students in a different environment than school and the classroom. Engaging with students during these informal activities give leaders opportunities to strengthen relationships as well as observe, listen, and learn from those who matter most in schools. More formal conversations regarding goals and progress proceed more smoothly when relationships and trust are strong. See Tool 1.3: Listening to Students for additional ways to access student voice to inform the learning agenda for the school.

5. Demonstrate a commitment to a trust-based culture

Building and sustaining trust is tricky, not because the relevant skills are difficult to develop, but because trust is in the perception of those we work with, not in us. It is not what we do as much as how others perceive us. Psencik (2011) writes, "Positive, high levels of trust in relationships with others and in organizations produce joy, effortless communication, transparent relationships, and high levels of energy," so it's worth the effort (p. 92). Covey (2008) states that organizations with low trust relationships have unhealthy working environments, hostility, guarded communications, defensiveness, and constant worry and suspicion (pp. 22–24).

Consider enacting the following practices to strengthen others' perceptions that you are trustworthy:

- Be honest and open. How many times have leaders in our nation gotten into trouble not because of what they did but because they lied about it? Remember that you as a principal are held to a high standard of character. Live up to it! Be as transparent as possible.

- Be positive. Let people know regularly that you believe in them and in the community's capacity to live up to expectations and to deliver its promise to children.

- Unleash talent. Share leadership responsibilities and give others the opportunity to develop their leadership skills. Build your own pipeline of learners and leaders.

- Share your personal mastery journey with all staff members. Engage others in understanding that you are a learner. Let them know that you are taking risks and it demands courage from you. Solicit staff's help in implementing innovative leadership approaches that keep students and staff engaged in the learning.

- Celebrate risk taking. Talk about the relationship between learning, changing, and risk taking. Acknowledge there is risk involved in any attempt at change. Discuss the risks the school undertakes when it adopts a new program or implements a new strategy.

- Apply risk-taking conversations to what happens in classrooms. Remind teachers you are there to support them in taking risks and that you do not expect all risks to produce desired results but you do expect all risks to result in learning.

CHAPTER 1

Reflections

- How do I demonstrate my intentional focus on learning for myself as well as for others?

- Am I viewed as a finisher? Are there pieces of my own equity and excellence agenda I have not addressed?

- Can my teams clearly articulate the value of team learning and how it supports improved student results?

- How do I connect others to the mission and promote learning and innovation to advance it?

- How are my actions intentionally informed by what I learn from students?

Each time a principal undertakes one of these actions, she offers another example of how her behavior aligns to her beliefs and she continues to build and maintain trust.

Conclusion

Achieving equity and excellence requires new ways of thinking and working. Yet imagining the changes required and actually trying them are very different. Educators are more likely to commit to change when they are led by a learning principal. They see they can take risks, make mistakes, and take on new challenges when their principal learns by their side. When learning leaders combine high expectations with high support and trust, next to nothing can stop them from achieving their goals.

References

Collins, J. & Porras, J. (1994). *Built to last: Successful habits of visionary companies.* HarperBusiness.

Covey, S. (2008). *The speed of trust.* Free Press.

Grissom, J.A. (2011). Can good principals keep teachers in disadvantaged schools? Linking principal effectiveness to teacher satisfaction and turnover in hard-to-staff environments. *Teachers College Record, 113*(11), 2552–2585.

Hirsh, S. & Killion, J. (2007). *The learning educator.* National Staff Development Council.

Hirsh, S. (2018). *4 cornerstones for professional learning: Fundamental principles pave the way for educators' actions.* Learning Forward. https://learning-forward.org/report/4-cornerstones/

Kegan, R. & Lahey, L. (2001). *How the way we talk can change the way we work.* Jossey-Bass.

Learning Forward. (2011). *Standards for Professional Learning.* Author.

Leithwood, K., Louis, K.S., Anderson, S., & Wahlstrom, K. (2004). *How leadership influences student learning.* The Wallace Foundation. Available at https://www.wallacefoundation.org/knowledge-center/pages/how-leadership-influences-student-learning.aspx

Manna, P. (2015). *Developing excellent school principals to advance teaching and learning: Considerations for state policy.* The Wallace Foundation. Available at https://www.wallacefoundation.org/knowledge-center/Documents/Developing-Excellent-School-Principals.pdf

Psencik, K. (2011). *The coach's craft: Powerful practices to support school leaders.* Learning Forward.

Schmidt, W. & Burroughs, N. (2013, Spring). Springing into life: How greater educational equality could grow from the Common Core mathematics standards. *American Educator,* 2–9.

TNTP. (2018). *The opportunity myth: What students can show us about how school is letting them down — and how to fix it.* [Website]. Available at https://tntp.org/publications/view/student-experiences/the-opportunity-myth

Tools index for Chapter 1

Tool	Title	Use
1.1	Running a Daily Self-check	This tool is a self-assessment for leaders to pause and determine how they want to present themselves to others.
1.2	Forming an Equity Mindset for Learning	This tool includes resources that principals and leadership teams can use for holding equity-focused conversations and planning sessions within school communities.
1.3	Supporting Learning Teams	This process helps principals facilitate discussion with leadership teams so they can identify opportunities for strengthening their approach to teaching and learning.
1.4	Listening to Students	This tool gives principals and leadership teams a process for learning about and practicing strategies for engaging with students to address issues at the school.

CHAPTER 2

Focusing on curriculum

Where are we now?

The principal's primary focus is equity and excellence for all students.

STRONGLY AGREE · AGREE · NO OPINION · DISAGREE · STRONGLY DISAGREE

The principal advocates for high-quality instructional materials with professional learning to support implementation.

STRONGLY AGREE · AGREE · NO OPINION · DISAGREE · STRONGLY DISAGREE

The principal establishes and protects learning team structures and time for deep study and planning for instruction.

STRONGLY AGREE · AGREE · NO OPINION · DISAGREE · STRONGLY DISAGREE

The principal addresses policies and practices that inhibit student access to high-quality teaching and learning.

STRONGLY AGREE · AGREE · NO OPINION · DISAGREE · STRONGLY DISAGREE

The principal systematically monitors student learning and assists learning teams in doing the same.

STRONGLY AGREE · AGREE · NO OPINION · DISAGREE · STRONGLY DISAGREE

www.learningforward.org

The LEARNING PRINCIPAL

CHAPTER 2

It is important that the principal is the lead learner in a school because that example sets the expectation among the staff for a learning culture. The principal's vision of continuous growth develops a culture in which all stakeholders are invested in new learning. When the principal is supportive of teachers' explorations of new practices, with that learning embedded within the teacher workday, the depth of learning and collaboration drastically increases. Acting as a co-learner, the principal raises the staff's collective responsibility to help all students achieve.

J.R. Ankenbruck
Principal, Mabel K. Holland Elementary School
Fort Wayne Community Schools
Fort Wayne, Indiana

Overview

Principals focused on equity for every student prioritize those aspects of schooling most likely to ensure that each student experiences meaningful learning daily, no matter which classroom they are assigned to and regardless of any aspect of their identity, be it race, gender, ethnicity, ability, or socioeconomic status.

The Professional Standards for Educational Leaders (NPBEA, 2015) establish that core work for school leaders includes leading curriculum, assessment, and instruction. Drawn from an expanding base of research, the Professional Standards for Educational Leaders (NPBEA, 2015) show that educational leaders influence student achievement by building ownership in the curriculum (p. 1). They create positive working conditions and ensure sufficient professional learning for all teams. They allocate resources purposefully, construct appropriate organizational systems, and engage in meaningful work in and outside of the classroom. Most important, highly effective principals stay focused on what students are expected to learn and keep careful track of their progress to address any concerns rapidly.

According to Standard 4 of the Professional Standards for Educational Leaders, effective leaders develop and support intellectually rigorous and coherent systems of curriculum, instruction, and assessment to promote each student's academic success and emotional and social well-being. And according to Standard 6, effective educational leaders develop the professional capacity and practice of school personnel to promote each student's academic success and well-being.

Principals are curriculum leaders in their schools. Driven by their moral purpose, they ensure that the ongoing study of curriculum and assessments

FOCUSING ON CURRICULUM

is grounded in the work of teacher learning teams through continuous improvement cycles. This chapter reviews the foundations for this important work and considers actions that learning principals take to leverage these responsibilities to advance equity and excellence in their schools.

The role of curriculum today

While educators have known for some time that the quality of teaching is the number one factor that influences student learning (Gordon, Kane, & Staiger, 2005; Rivkin et al., 2005), until recently they were not as familiar with the research regarding the contribution of instructional materials (Boser et al., 2015; Chingos & Whitehurst, 2012; Steiner, 2017). "When all classrooms are filled with high-quality instructional materials, students are more likely to learn" (Learning Forward, 2018). Many education organizations now provide tools and resources for identifying high-quality standards-aligned curriculum and instructional materials and distinguishing them from others. See the organization EdReports (https://www.edreports.org/), and these resources: Instructional Materials Evaluation Tool (https://achievethecore.org/page/1946/instructional-materials-evaluation-tool), and Educators Evaluating the Quality of Instructional Products (https://www.achieve.org/our-initiatives/equip/equip). Principals have limited excuses for not ensuring their teachers have access to great materials as well as the tools and expertise to select them.

Effective use of curriculum requires teachers who understand it deeply and use it with intentionality and professional judgment, based on their particular context and the needs of their students (Learning Forward, 2018). "Frequent and ongoing professional development is needed to support teachers in understanding, internalizing, and effectively using curriculum"

(Instruction Partners, 2017, p. 10). Schools get the most from professional development for teachers when they invest in job-embedded professional learning that supports teacher implementation of high-quality curriculum (Taylor et al., 2015; Toon & Jensen, 2017; Wiener & Pimentel, 2017).

Learning principals are aware that teachers regularly supplement and modify any curriculum they are provided. The National Council for Teachers of Mathematics (2014) found that teachers of marginalized students focus primarily on rote skills and procedures with little attention to meaningful mathematics learning. When students who are marginalized only receive such rote instruction, that discrepancy in instructional practices deepens any opportunity gap. In mathematics, as well as other subject areas, teachers aspire to equitable learning by developing conceptual understanding of all students with a particular focus on those students who are marginalized.

Professional learning anchored in curriculum

The Standards for Professional Learning (Learning Forward, 2011) state, "the body of research about effective schools identifies collaboration and professional learning as two characteristics that consistently appear in schools that substantially increase student learning" (p. 16). Learning teams or professional learning communities (PLCs) are among the most common learning designs used in schools. Learning principals are keenly aware that not all PLCs are created equal. Without a purposeful agenda, intentional support and structures, and leaders knowledgeable about college- and career-ready standards, learning teams do not achieve their intended outcomes.

Anchoring the team learning cycle in the study of curriculum combines the two factors with the greatest potential to ensure high-quality teaching and learning for all students — professional learning and high-quality materials. The learning cycle begins with educators carefully examining data including student work in order to inform goal setting to drive student and educator learning. Thoughtful data analysis can help learning teams pinpoint the student standards and units where students and teachers struggle most to guide the development of learning goals. Learning teams can realistically undertake deep study and potential modification of two to four units per year and these initial stages of the learning team cycle ensure they focus in the right direction.

The next stages of the cycle involve educators intensively studying the student standards and concepts addressed in particular instructional units; careful review, preparation, and practice for the most challenging lessons; and sustained classroom-based support for educators when implementation of their learning begins.

One instructional challenge for effective principals is guiding the review and revision of assessment tools (e.g. daily check-ins, tests, essays, projects, and presentations). How does the principal ensure that all assessments that teaching teams use provide reliable information about student progress? Most high-quality curriculum materials will incorporate such tasks; however, not all teachers have access to such materials. There is often a strong rationale for revising and adapting assessments. Because useful assessments are challenging to write, teaching teams and the principal may need to study how to effectively design them. Aligned assessments give teaching teams the best opportunity to make reliable inferences to design instruction that meets the needs of their students.

When principals systematically facilitate teams in analyzing student standards and their curriculum materials, deeply understanding the concepts, and

developing reliable assessments, they have a school-based, coherent curriculum essential for student success. This coherence enables teams to explore varieties of purposeful, intriguing lesson plans that lead students to full engagement and involvement in their learning.

Barriers to equity and excellence

Principals are motivated to address equity when presented with research and evidence regarding the important role that curriculum and high-quality instructional materials play in student results. However, school and system leaders must transform long-standing assumptions and systemic practices for principals to assume greater leadership and responsibility for the materials used in their schools.

Principals may not lead curriculum work in schools because of the enduring practice that curriculum is managed outside the school. Many people in the district play a significant role in the selection and evaluation of curriculum and materials; however, learning principals recognize that the school is where they are used. Therefore, principals' perspectives are essential in the curriculum selection and implementation processes. Principals may also not lead curriculum work because they lack skills in this area. Unfortunately, too few have experienced professional learning to support their leadership with this responsibility. Without significant principal leadership, however, teachers often engage passively in equity-focused curriculum work.

Another major challenge is where principals spend their time. In recent studies conducted on how principals spend time, only about 8% was spent in the classroom. In a 2006 study, principals reported spending the largest proportion of their time (35%) on motivating teachers, 24% on reporting and

FOCUSING ON CURRICULUM

Empowering teachers through collective responsibility

Teacher teams at Mabel K. Holland Elementary formatively assess students using rigorous short assessments two to three times a month. Their collaborative analysis of these student artifacts, first of all, drives forthcoming instruction for each teaching team. Second, the frequency of the assessments allows teachers to cycle through different standards multiple times throughout the year. Finally, by following this sequence, teams can check student progress and give students targeted, small-group instruction numerous times. Throughout this process my role as principal is to balance the art of empowering, questioning, and motivating teachers. It is important that I work collaboratively with team members, not as an evaluator, but as a peer who is invested in student success.

Before they begin planning instruction, teacher teams work with the instructional coach and me to identify formative assessments and exemplars. We understand the importance of choosing an assessment that precisely measures the taught standard at its highest level, which requires students to think critically and problem solve. We also learned that assessing at that level could lead us make to changes in planning and instruction. By identifying the assessment before planning instruction, teachers increase the level of rigor in their instruction. They can see that not all students show initial mastery of high-level critical thinking so the teachers adjust their instruction until all students are able to grasp the concept. The purpose of the assessments is to guide future instruction in the classroom and monitor student progress in critical thinking.

After they assess student performance, the teacher teams, in collaboration with the instructional coach and me, analyze the artifacts using the exemplar for guidance. We do that analysis with the understanding that, in most cases, the team will spiral back to the standard taught later in the school year. For now, the team is

Principal J.R. Ankenbruck helps a student sharpen critical thinking skills.

looking for general student understanding, common errors, student specific misunderstandings, and most importantly, the student's ability to critically think and problem solve. The team's analysis will determine whether they use small-group instruction to address student needs or try reteaching to a larger group. When teachers regularly analyze student work through this lens, they gain better understanding of their students' strengths and challenges.

I make sure that teachers understand that I don't expect initial student mastery because of the increased rigor; however, I do expect that they will use evidence of what each student knows and doesn't know to adjust their instruction. I empower teachers to trust their judgment and take risks when changing their instruction to address identified student needs. Such empowerment and trust, I believe, creates teacher ownership of student learning and results — and that ownership is a key factor in student success.

— *J.R. Ankenbruck*

CHAPTER 2

compliance, and 20% on discipline, with all three areas accounting for 77% of their time (MetLife Inc., 2006). In a 2009 study of Miami-Dade County Public Schools, Florida, principals spent 54% of their time in the school office. Another 40% of their time was spent around the campus in hallways, on playgrounds, and in cafeterias (Horng, Klasik, & Loeb, 2009).

Finally, ensuring that teachers have access to high-quality instructional materials does not necessarily ensure that students have access. In addition to the challenges teachers may face in trying to scaffold instruction so that students can work on grade level, policies and procedures may inhibit student access to teachers and classes that prepare them for college and careers. Some of these practices have occurred for so long that they have become invisible to many. Learning principals are vehement about confronting barriers and advocating for all students taking challenging curriculum.

Taking action

Consider the following actions that learning principals take to leverage their responsibilities in curriculum, assessment, and instruction to advance equity and excellence in their schools.

1. Advocate for high-quality instructional materials

Learning principals are aware of all core curriculum and instructional materials used in classrooms in their schools. They lead regular curriculum reviews to ensure that teachers and students have the quality and number of materials they need to ground the learning for the year. When they find that materials are misaligned to course- or grade-level standards or not meeting specific needs such as being culturally

responsive to students, learning principals demand that new resources be identified and provided to give teachers the foundational tools they need to ensure effective instruction.

Learning principals stay up to date about various sources of high-quality materials. When teams or individual teachers are struggling, principals are able to point them to sources for validated inexpensive and free resources that may help them.

They pay particular attention to their less experienced staff or members with new teaching assignments and ensure first they have the materials as well as the professional support they will need to get off to a good start.

Learning principals are also aware that high-quality instructional materials are not equally accessible for all courses and subjects. As a result, they ensure that those teams with access to fewer validated resources are provided professional learning in how to select and verify that instructional materials meet course standards and grade level intent. Those teams are given additional support to edit or write lessons that meet grade-level standards and promote the outcomes they seek for their students. See Tool 2.1: Inventorying the Curriculum to support your oversight responsibility for ensuring high-quality instructional materials in the hands of all teachers.

2. Know the curriculum

Learning principals are true instructional leaders. As they take on the responsibility of assisting teachers in using the curriculum well, learning principals need first to understand the curriculum itself. Effective principals spend time studying the district's curriculum and materials. They participate in district-level curriculum selection and design work. While principals will never know deeply all content standards being

FOCUSING ON CURRICULUM

taught by teams in their buildings, they can know how curriculum is structured, what distinguishes a high-quality curriculum, what constitutes the component parts of a high-quality curriculum, and what is the relationship of high-quality curriculum to instruction and assessment. Each of these skills is essential to fulfilling their responsibility for leading curriculum implementation at their schools (Glatthorn, Jailall, & Jailall, 2017).

Next, when they begin to apply their new knowledge and skills in their individual schools, learning principals insist that learning teams spend their time analyzing curriculum and curriculum materials. Yet developing deep curriculum understanding is a challenge. If principals hold back because they lack understanding of curriculum or they perceive themselves as having inadequate expertise, the teacher learning teams may be reluctant to dig into the curriculum and thus are unlikely to come to an understanding about it themselves. Principals cannot be experts in every content area, but they can develop the observation, facilitation, and coaching skills that promote deeper learning and application among teachers. Using designs such as observations and classroom walkthroughs, learning principals can use tools to collect data about how teachers are implementing curriculum in grade level and subject matter (see Tool 2.2: Conducting a Curriculum Walkthrough). By developing a set of thought-provoking questions, principals can act as coaches to teams or individual teachers so they might design and teach more effective lessons and units. Principals, in communities or individually, might consider asking teachers questions like these:

- Where do we expect the students to be at the end of this unit or year?
- Where are the students now? How do we know?
- How do we know how students are progressing throughout the year?

- What instructional strategies recommended in the curriculum are new to us? How will we test or practice them with this group?
- What do we need to learn to do differently?

These and other questions keep the team focused on the learning cycle while at the same time reminding them of the importance of their work.

3. Promote conceptual understanding in learning team discussions

Learning principals know their presence in learning teams is important. Consistently showing up demonstrates the priority the principal places on this task. Learning principals use this time to push teachers to deeper thinking and learning. They can ask questions that promote deeper appreciation for the learning cycle. And they can facilitate conversations that promote conceptual learning. Conceptual understanding is the "Why" behind any skill: "Why do I need to know how to organize my writing? Because all authors organize their writing so that they best communicate what they want the reader to understand." When students know the "why," they accelerate their learning because it is easier to see the meaning behind the skill.

• • •

A strong curriculum leader, Kathy Larson, retired principal of Heritage Elementary in Woodburn, Oregon, was working with a group of 3rd-grade teachers on conceptual understanding. She kept prodding the team to think about the big ideas — the enduring understandings — in their social studies/ELA integrated units as they were working on their year-long curriculum map. They were focused on the Lewis and Clark expedition, which especially affected the growth of Oregon. As a result of her persistent prodding and exploration of the materials, the team finally recognized where she was headed. "What we really want students to understand is that perspectives matter in what authors write; their experiences, their points of view, the times in which they lived all shape those perspectives. We annually teach students about the Lewis and Clark expedition. We focus on their diary, the struggles they experienced, the amazing discoveries they made as they journeyed west. We seldom consider the story from the Salmon People's point of view. We want to change that!"

Larson said, "Wow, you really have deep understanding of how the author's perspective shapes his or her writing. Wonder how we can help students understand that concept?"

The principal was aware that the district materials that the teachers used were weak and teachers were constantly having to locate or write new lessons to fill gaps. After they struggled a bit longer, the team was able to write three powerful units of study for the year with three essential questions all grounded in one conceptual and student-learning standard:

Unit 1: What impacts an author's writings over time?

Unit 2: How have authors' points of view affected our thinking?

Unit 3: How has the telling of history shaped history?

Those questions would have never been written if it had not been for the principal prodding that team to think more deeply about the underlying concepts to convey to students.

• • •

Principals can challenge all staff members to clarify concepts embedded in the curriculum. They can host deeper conversations around the concepts that form the content standards. Many curriculum documents do not explicitly state the concepts to be learned, even though the intent is for students to develop conceptual understanding. Teachers cannot address concepts fully with students that they do not fully understand themselves. Learning principals know the importance of the learning cycle stage that calls for teachers to answer the questions, "What do students need to know and be able to do to achieve the intended goals?" and "What do you as educators

> ## Arizona Principals Form Learning Community
>
> Principals can hone knowledge of curriculum and their curriculum analysis skills by participating in a community of learning principals.
>
> When Mesa [Arizona] Public Schools introduced a new curriculum and instructional materials, principals realized the challenges they were going to face during implementation. As they began to talk among themselves, two participants in the Arizona Learning Leaders for Learning Schools initiative invited other principals to join them as members of a learning community. Six principals began hosting regular meetings focused on their roles and responsibilities as curriculum leaders.
>
> Great ideas kept emerging. One outcome was a plan to support learning and implementation across their schools. They organized cross-school learning communities by grade levels to focus on deliberate study of student content standards and instructional strategies embedded in the new curriculum. They explored different approaches to helping teachers implement the curriculum and how to support them throughout the year.

FOCUSING ON CURRICULUM

need to understand and be able to do to ensure they are successful?" When principals ask such questions, they move teams closer to clarifying the concepts to be learned. Rarely is sufficient attention given to that second question. Learning principals focus attention there because they know that teacher learning is key to student learning. See Tool 2.3: Leveraging the Curriculum Work of Learning Communities for guidance with supporting conceptual understandings by teachers.

4. Make learning accessible

Learning principals are continually focused on the creation of conditions that best support teaching and learning. They consider several questions, such as "How do we ensure that our most experienced, most productive teachers teach our most challenged students?" "How do we guarantee that those students who are often underrepresented in our school's most academic challenging curriculum are accessing it and doing well?" "How do we ensure adequate time for learning?" "What classroom schedule supports student and staff job-embedded learning?" "What support systems will there be for students falling below expectations?"

To ensure that all students have access to teaching and curriculum, learning principals examine disciplinary practices that result in students losing valuable class time and falling further behind their peers. They invest in social-emotional learning practices and access supports from the growing number of organizations with expertise in this area. In high-performing schools, principals facilitate teaching teams to develop strategies for keeping students in class. Principals work with teachers and support staff, such as interventionists and special education teachers, to "push in" to the classroom to guarantee that they are doing all they can to keep all students connected to the instructional core at grade level. Principals help teachers develop skills in building relationships with students and giving them space to learn appropriate behaviors in class. The more frequently that students are removed from classroom sessions, the further behind they get in mastering grade-level curriculum. Principals are key to every student excelling.

Learning principals ensure that students who might not have the requisite skills they need to succeed in class are supported by classroom teachers who differentiate and scaffold learning for them. Principals work with learning teams to identify and learn those strategies that enable below-grade-level students to do grade-level work. They consider flexible scheduling that allows for students to prepare or gain readiness for more challenging work, including double-block periods for advanced mathematics and adopting programs like AVID, which gives every student an advocate while teaching them college-ready skills. Collaborative strategies may include engaging community partners who are inspirational for students who are reticent or reluctant to try more challenging work or building collaborative environments within large group classes. Principals focused on learning build in time for complex or multitiered instructional support approaches such as counseling, enrichment, Response to Intervention, extra support, college- and career planning, and work internships. They also use technology and online courses as appropriate (Psencik, 2009). The potential to support learning for all students increases when principals choose to try nontraditional scheduling options.

Access to advanced coursework is another benchmark for equity-focused leaders. Effective secondary school leaders remove major roadblocks that have traditionally been gatekeepers to keep some students out of advanced classes, in particular, students of

Focus on standards and curriculum leads to improved student results

When I took over as principal of Santa Fe High School, I noticed that teachers did not connect to their curriculum or standards. The district had created curriculum processes but teachers would complain that they already knew what worked best for their students. I investigated further and noticed that teachers began lesson planning with activities they liked without looking at learning objectives or linking activities to standards. I also found that when teachers attempted to differentiate learning activities, they tended to create entertaining activities, rather than ones tied to standards.

To create structures that would help us sharpen our focus on standards and curriculum, I arranged the high school schedule to prioritize and establish times for teachers to meet in professional learning communities (PLCs). In short coaching cycles of two to four weeks, teachers focused on three major areas: student assessments, aligning curriculum and instruction to standards, and analyzing student work. Participants in the coaching cycles included teachers, instructional coaches, and the administration, all following specific learning designs. In the first work phase, our purpose was to connect curriculum processes with aligned standards and assessments. First, teams needed to analyze old instructional practices for value and worth. For example, English teachers read *To Kill a Mockingbird* using instruction that taught about the time period, unjust prejudices, and an unfair legal system, yet showed little student growth on assessments. After teachers participated in PLCs with a standards-based learning design focused on characterization and inferencing, they were able to use the text to support student understanding of characterization and making inferences.

In their teams, teachers also researched and chose learning designs. Based on the district curriculum focus, their first learning design analyzed power standards in the curriculum with assessments. Assessments became shorter and more rigorous. Teachers identified power standards and took the time to understand the depth and complexity of each one. We administrators and instructional coaches posed questions such as, "What nouns represent the content and how might the verbs tell the action students must perform?" "What is the level of rigor required of students in the standard?" Their responses showed that teachers were beginning to plan with the end in mind — the student performance they expected to see. And they grasped the level of rigor needed to align instruction and assessments with state standards.

Principal Rachel Harris (foreground) facilitates a PLC at Santa Fe High School.

The second work phase, led by the leadership team, required more time and the most change from teachers. This learning design focused on aligning their unit lessons and weekly instruction to the standards. First, I asked them to focus on one or two standards and set specific SMART (Strategic/Specific, Measurable, Attainable, Results oriented, Time bound) student learning goals. Teachers next used a KASAB (Knowledge, Attitude, Skill, Aspiration, Behavior) protocol to identify barriers they would face in teaching the unit. Teams were held accountable for planning what they would need to know or be able to do to address identified issues, and they tapped strengths of team members to overcome obstacles. Finally, we began coaching cycles. I posed questions to help teachers develop their understanding of the standards and the curriculum.

After completing coaching cycles, teachers began making instructional shifts. To support these shifts, they

FOCUSING ON CURRICULUM

identified sound, relevant resources they could use to address student expectations. This was the climactic point of teacher learning: As they taught the lesson in their classrooms, teachers received specific feedback from teammates. Afterward, drawing on the feedback and assessment data, teachers analyzed student work samples. By analyzing student work, teams could see where students progressed toward achieving specific SMART goals. Examining student work also allowed teachers to reflect on and refine their instructional approaches. After several cycles, teachers routinely paid attention to the standards and identified viable curriculum and instructional approaches.

Within one year of shifting to focused attention on curriculum alignment and instruction, Santa Fe High School increased state testing scores by 17 points. As a result, the leadership and teacher teams reaffirmed their commitment to short coaching cycles within professional learning communities. We attribute our recent success to this commitment and share the belief that it will contribute to future success for students.

— *Rachel Harris*

Stage 1 Analyze data	Stage 2 Identify barriers and plan assessments	Stage 3 Plan instruction	Stage 4 Implement instruction	Stage 5 Analysis of student work
Date:	Date:	Date:	Date:	Date:
Finalize student goal setting from learning design: • Create SMART goal on standards-based assessment (SBA) or unit-based assessment (UBA) • Use the KASAB method to identify barriers	Ensure that we have a good, solid assessment: • Use "peeling back the layers" learning design Or, for UBA: • Learning design: Writing reliable and valid tests	What do we need to learn in order to teach this to the level we need to? Who is responsible for what by next week? • Use learning design: Designing effective aligned lessons	Implement instruction and begin identifying the next goal for the following SBA or UBA	Analyze student data from SBA or UBA to reflect on goal. Use student work samples and coaching information to decide on improvements: • Modify learning design: Tuning protocol
Notes (e.g. discussion, evidence):				

color and those who live in poverty. The secondary principal monitors enrollment in advanced curriculum, such as AP and honors classes. They make sure those classes have full enrollment and that students who are in them mirror the racial and economic make-up of the student population. Principals also work with teacher learning teams to ensure they have the skills to meet the needs of all their students so none drop out of advanced classes. When students are falling behind, principals assist teaching teams in scaffolding and differentiating instructional approaches. When students seem disinterested, principals inspire teaching teams to entice students into the learning with culturally responsive engagement and instructional strategies.

Learning principals are comfortable in confronting implicit biases appropriately. When principals combat biases, they nurture the staff to believe that poverty and race are not predictors of student success. They guide all staff to believe that they are change agents for educational equity. Principals constantly remind staff members that their commitment is to ensure that all students leave school having risen to rigorous grade-level standards and gained confidence in their value and abilities. To honor that commitment, all staff ultimately shift their attitudes to foster equity and excellence.

5. Monitor relentlessly

Monitoring student learning systematically and regularly is an essential skill of all effective principals (see sidebar, p. 27). As principals focus on the learning communities in their schools, positive collaboration results, and this energy is essential to the continuous monitoring of student achievement. If principals foster the concept that data is information teaching teams use to focus their instructional plans, teachers

experience the relationship between student learning and their own.

Learning principals establish systems for data collection and analysis and schedule data sessions with each team at the beginning of each new learning cycle. Hirsh and Crow (2018) propose a 12-week cycle in *Becoming a Learning Team* (pp. 23–24). This cycle engages learning teams in five stages of work: analyzing student data, setting goals for themselves and their students, designing their own learning, implementing what they are learning, and monitoring and adjusting. Through this learning cycle, teaching teams and their principals discover what they and their students are learning and creatively plan for new learning for themselves and their students. They return to analyzing their data and student work, and the cycle begins again.

Teachers are able to monitor student progress because they develop a road map early in the cycle with their learning agendas and assessments. During the goal-setting phase, principals help teams pinpoint the key standards and concepts that students must master during an upcoming unit. Before they look for student progress on those standards, team members recheck their assessments, standard by standard, to ensure they have sufficient reliable information to make judgments about what students are learning and what changes they need to make in their plans. This may sound like an overwhelming task. Teaching teams who do it, however, know about their students and their progress, so they naturally differentiate their instruction and scaffolding as needed.

Learning principals showcase and celebrate student learning. Using data to drive instructional decisions is a key step in the cycle. Doing it well matters. And although monitoring is essential, showcasing the learning sends a powerful message

FOCUSING ON CURRICULUM

Effective Principals Rigorously Track Student Data

During sessions of the Galveston County [Texas] Learning Leaders community of practice, principal Rachel Harris often discussed with her principal community members how she thought her students would perform on the state ELA assessments at the end of the year.

Her counterparts asked her, "Do you really think your students will be as successful as you say the data is predicting?"

Harris shared, "I know how they will do because I have been monitoring their progress monthly!"

The data proved her right.

When Texas state assessment results came in at the end of the school year, Santa Fe High School had moved from a "Very Low" to "Very High" rating.

to the school community that learning is core work. Teaching teams may post bar graphs or class progress charts by their doors to make student learning visible. Student work is featured in the hallways.

The authors worked with a staff that had a circular media center in the middle of the school building. The principal took the lead in telling a year-long learning story. Month by month, she posted student work, pictures of students working together, pictures of teachers in their learning communities all around the media center. Students and staff, as well as parents and community partners who visited the school, saw the learning as it progressed. All those images purposefully showed the significance of student and staff learning together throughout the year. See Tool 2.4: Monitoring the Learning Cycle for ideas related to designing systems of support.

Conclusion

When principals prioritize what evidence indicates makes significant differences in schools, they put students and equity first. The quality of the instructional materials in use in classrooms and the quality of the professional learning available to educators are two factors that effective instructional leaders emphasize.

A recent report about Washington DC Public Schools' LEAP program and efforts to increase student success, found that the most effective professional learning is school-based and content-specific, grounded in instructional materials, and focused on strategies that teachers use with their students (Learning Forward, 2019). In the LEAP program, teachers have dedicated time for inquiry-oriented collaboration and study to deeply understand the content and concepts embedded in the curriculum they use with students.

Takeaways from that LEAP study offer principals and other school leaders ideas about how to make them a reality in their schools:

- Teacher effectiveness increases through professional learning cycles focused on student content and instructional materials.
- Implementing high-quality instructional materials is complex and requires intensive support for educators.
- Alignment of an instructional vision throughout a system is bolstered through collaboration with an external assistance provider.
- Key enabling conditions for success include a plan for intentional scaling and intentional development of leaders throughout a system.
- Educators who implemented LEAP with high fidelity saw marked improvements in student results (Learning Forward, 2019).

Reflections

- What new ideas and practices from this chapter will I share with my leadership team?

- In what ways will I strengthen my knowledge and skills in leading and facilitating others in using high-quality curriculum materials to increase equity and high levels of performance of all students?

- How will I use my own goal-setting process to plan my way to success? How will I interact with my peers to support my own learning?

- What evidence will I accept to demonstrate my own progress in shifting my own practices? How will I showcase my learning and celebrate with staff and students?

- How will I address implicit biases that may be active in my school?

Implementing these key findings with fidelity is a result of intentional curriculum leadership on the part of the principal. From understanding curriculum and curriculum materials, to facilitating teams in analyzing curriculum materials, aligning assessments, designing powerful instructional practices, to analyzing student work, the principal takes the lead and engages in ways that reflects that in this school, everyone learns.

References

Boser, U., Chingos, M., & Straus, C. (2015). *The hidden value of curriculum reform.* Center for American Progress. Available at https://www.americanprogress.org/issues/education-k-12/reports/2015/10/14/122810/the-hidden-value-of-curriculum-reform/

Chingos, M. & Whitehurst, R.G. (2012). *Choosing blindly: Instructional materials, teacher effectiveness, and the Common Core.* Brookings Institution. Available at https://www.brookings.edu/research/choosing-blindly-instructional-materials-teacher- effectiveness-and-the-common-core/

Glatthorn, A., Jailall, J. M., & Jailall, J. K. (2017). *Principal as a curriculum leader.* Corwin.

Gordon, R., Kane, T. J., & Staiger, D. O. (2006, April). Identifying effective teachers using performance on the job. *Hamilton Project Discussion Paper.* Brookings Institution. Available at https://www.hamiltonproject.org/assets/legacy/files/downloads_and_links/Identifying_Effective_Teachers_Using_Performance_on_the_Job.pdf

Hirsh, S. & Crow, T. (2018). *Becoming a learning team: A guide to a teacher-led cycle of continuous improvement* (2nd ed.). Learning Forward.

Horng, E.L., Klasik, D. & Loeb, S. (2009). *Principal time-use and school effectiveness. CALDER Working Paper No. 34.* National Center of Analysis of Longitudinal Data in Education Research, Urban Institute.

Instruction Partners. (2017). *What does it take to implement a strong curriculum effectively: Part one: What do we know about the experience*

FOCUSING ON CURRICULUM

of schools implementing rigorous curricula? Author. Available at https://static1.squarespace.com/static/589d1b9ebe65941098d57d14/t/5a25c092419202d42eb86600/1512423571971/IP+Curriculum+White+Paper+FINAL.pdf

Learning Forward. (2018). *High-quality curricula and team-based professional learning: A perfect partnership for equity.* Author. https://learningforward.org/report/high-quality-curricula-and-team-based-professional-learning-a-perfect-partnership-for-equity/

Learning Forward. (2019). *The path to instructional excellence and equitable outcomes.* Author. https://learningforward.org/report/the-path-to-instructional-excellence-and-equitable-outcomes/

Learning Forward. (2011). *Standards for Professional Learning.* Author.

MetLife Inc. (2006, September). *The MetLife survey of the American teacher: Expectations and experiences. A survey of teachers, principals and leaders of college education programs.* ED496558. Available at https://eric.ed.gov/?q=MetLife+teacher+survey+2006&id=ED496558

National Council of Teachers of Mathematics. (2014). *Principles to actions: Ensuring mathematical success for all.* Author.

National Policy Board for Educational Administration (NPBEA) (2015). *Professional Standards for Educational Leaders.* Author.

Psencik, K. (2009). *Accelerating student and staff learning: Purposeful curriculum collaboration.* Corwin.

Rivkin, S.G., Hanushek, E.A., & Kain, J.F. (2005). *Teachers, schools, and academic achievement.* University of Texas-Dallas Schools Project. Available at http://hanushek.stanford.edu/sites/default/files/publications/Rivkin%2BHanushek%2BKain%202005%20Ecta%2073%282%29.pdf

Tools index for Chapter 2

Tool	Title	Use
2.1	Inventorying the Curriculum	This tool, a survey-and-inventory process, identifies the availability of high-quality instructional materials and teacher accessibility to them.
2.2	Conducting a Curriculum Walkthrough	This tool gives examples of curriculum-specific observation tools, which can be adapted to collect data about classroom teaching practices.
2.3	Leveraging the Curriculum Work of Learning Communities	This tool helps focus teacher teams on the study, assessment, and implementation of high-quality instructional materials.
2.4	Monitoring the Learning Cycle	This tool supports principals and members of teacher teams in collectively monitoring learning cycles.

Steiner, D. (2017, March). *Curriculum research: What we know and where we need to go.* Standards-Work. Available at https://standardswork.org/wp-content/uploads/2017/03/sw-curriculum-research-report-fnl.pdf

Taylor, J.A., Getty S.R., Kowalski, S.M., Wilson, C.D., Carlson, J., & Van Scotter, P. (2015). An efficacy trial of research-based curriculum materials with curriculum-based professional development. *American Educational Research Journal, 52*(5), 984–1017.

Toon, D. & Jensen, B. (2017). *Teaching our teachers: A better way: Using K–12 curriculum to improve teacher preparation.* Learning First. Available at https://learningfirst.com/wp-content/uploads/2020/07/15.-Using-K-12-curriculum-to-imprve-teacher-preparation.pdf

Wiener, R. & Pimentel, S. (2017). *Practice what you teach: Connecting curriculum and professional learning in schools.* Aspen Institute. Available at https://assets. aspeninstitute.org/content/uploads/2017/04/Practice-What-You-Teach.pdf

CHAPTER
3

Managing change

Where are we now?

The principal understands change theory and how to manage the process and impacts of change upon staff.

STRONGLY AGREE · AGREE · NO OPINION · DISAGREE · STRONGLY DISAGREE

The principal uses change tools when planning and implementing new initiatives and programs.

STRONGLY AGREE · AGREE · NO OPINION · DISAGREE · STRONGLY DISAGREE

The principal uses a logic model to guide the improvement agenda.

STRONGLY AGREE · AGREE · NO OPINION · DISAGREE · STRONGLY DISAGREE

The principal appreciates the role of stakeholder engagement to ensure successful change.

STRONGLY AGREE · AGREE · NO OPINION · DISAGREE · STRONGLY DISAGREE

The principal builds a culture where change is celebrated.

STRONGLY AGREE · AGREE · NO OPINION · DISAGREE · STRONGLY DISAGREE

CHAPTER 3

The ultimate goal of an educator is to develop lifelong learners. This goal holds true equally for the students and adults in a school. As a school leader, I believe part of my job is to inspire people around me to push themselves — and, in turn, the entire school staff — to learn continuously and find a better way to do things. If we are to do this, I must show them the way by doing it myself. When students and teachers see the principal learning alongside them, they have a model of the continuous improvement process. They can look at me and say, "Well, if she can do it, I can do it!" Leading by example gives others a path they can follow toward deeper learning, improved practice, and stronger performance.

Lindsay Amstutz-Martin
Principal, Fairfield Elementary
Fort Wayne Community Schools
Fort Wayne, Indiana

Overview

As recent events across the world demonstrate, principals, along with other leaders in education systems, have the frequent challenge of managing and supporting change efforts. Such efforts may be in response to unexpected events; often, principals are leaders in initiating change to make a positive difference for students. Teachers, parents, students, members of the community, and others depend on the school leader to help guide them through the nuances associated with change.

Often change can come without warning:

- A superintendent unexpectedly retires resulting in new district leadership.
- A new state or provincial policy leaves everyone scrambling for help implementing.
- A tragedy or crisis (such as a pandemic) causes everything to be turned upside down during a critical point in the school year.

At other times, principals expect or initiate the change and have adequate time to prepare their staff, whether they are selecting and implementing a new curriculum or engineering a broader school improvement effort. Even in these cases, staff require time to effectively engage in a change process. While some will eagerly anticipate a given change, others will actively resist it or mourn what was. In some places change is nonnegotiable and urgent; in others it is necessary but perhaps not perceived as urgent.

One thing is certain: "…[T]here are virtually no documented instances of troubled schools being turned around without intervention by a powerful leader. Many other factors may contribute to such turnarounds, but leadership is the catalyst" (Leithwood, Seashore-Louis, Anderson, & Wahlstrom, 2004). No matter the context, learning principals recognize the various ways staff engage in change processes and create systems to help them navigate it.

Shirley Hord and James Roussin (2013) proposed six beliefs about change that serve as the foundation for the concepts and recommendations presented in this chapter:
1. All change requires learning, and improvement requires change.
2. Implementing a change through social action increases potential for success.
3. Individuals change before the school changes.
4. Change affects the emotional and behavioral dimensions of people.
5. People opt for change when they foresee potential for enhancing their work.
6. A change leader's role is to facilitate conversations that invite others to own the desired change. (pp. 2–3)

In essence, they propose that all change ultimately entails new learning, and while change is very personal, it's most effective when done in collaboration with others. This chapter explores how leaders can create the conditions and learning opportunities to help their staff navigate change. It also focuses on the importance of establishing readiness for change as well as strategies to help staff emerge from a change process successfully. Because principals do not talk about "making change" in isolation from a strategy, this chapter uses the terms *innovation, new program,* and *initiative* as proxies for change.

Making change is complex

Often when facilitating conversations about change, the authors show a video produced by Smarter Every Day. In the clip, welders create a bicycle with a front wheel that turns to the left when the handlebars are turned to the right. It is described as a "backwards bicycle," and the star of the video, Destin, sets out to learn how to ride it. Viewers are often surprised how long it takes for Destin to learn how to ride the backwards bike. After practicing almost every day, he finally masters it in eight months. He's surprised by how the slightest distraction (like his cell phone ringing in his pocket) causes him to lose his focus on the task of learning to ride.

At one point in the video, Destin makes the point that knowledge does not equal understanding. He recognizes that he knows the concepts required to ride this unusual bike, but his brain doesn't fully have the understanding. The same holds true for school settings — knowledge doesn't always equal understanding. Often, learners know "what" a change might entail, but they don't have a deep understanding of what that means for them personally, procedurally, or organizationally. Lacking full understanding can be a barrier for implementing the vision of the change learners are trying to achieve.

https://www.youtube.com/watch?v=MFzDaBzBIL0

Consider the many changes that educators potentially face. They may have to teach to new state standards using new curricula and instructional materials. They experience changes to the accountability and testing requirements. Districts may roll out new safety procedures. Students may face changes

CHAPTER 3

in the Code of Conduct, and parents may have to get used to new processes for being involved in their children's education. Change is constant. Like Destin and the backwards bicycle, there are still many distractions that take people back to their comfortable ways of operating.

In their seminal text, *Leadership on the Line: Staying Alive Through the Dangers of Leading,* Ron Heifetz and Marty Linsky (2002) describe the differences between technical and adaptive challenges. Technical challenges, they argue, are often easy to identify and can be solved with tried and true solutions. Often the solutions can be implemented quickly. Adaptive challenges, on the other hand, require innovative thinking and may require change at multiple levels within the organization. Because of their complex nature, schools are places where adaptive challenges, and changes, are more the norm than the exception. Building principals are charged with supporting their staff members through those complex changes.

Change is a big deal, and principals cannot leave it to chance that their staff — or themselves personally — will embark successfully on a change process. Learning principals are intentional about planning to manage change. This could include that they develop strategies to gauge the readiness of their staff to engage in the change process, create support systems and structures, and celebrate appropriately throughout the change process.

A change plan is essential

Every school improvement, curriculum adoption, or program implementation plan requires change by individuals and organizations. Successful management of change relies on a number of factors. Fortunately, years of study and attention to the change process have resulted in substantive guidance and resources to support change within schools. When engaging in a change process, the authors ask leaders and their teams to consider the following questions:

1. What is the current situation (problem of practice) that needs attention? How was it identified?

2. What is the potential solution or innovation? What research supports it?

3. What is the outcome sought? What will it look like when the desired results are achieved?

4. What will staff and stakeholders need to learn and be able to do differently to achieve the desired results?

5. How will people acquire the new knowledge and skills?

6. How will progress be monitored and follow-through provided to ensure success? How will effectiveness be measured?

Answers to all these questions are used to inform a theory of change and logic model (explained in more detail below) for supporting the change process.

1. What is the current situation, or problem of practice, that needs attention? How was it identified?

Making change does not necessarily result in improving practice. School leaders and staff need to understand the underlying problem to instructional issues; otherwise, they will not likely achieve the outcomes they expect. A learning principal collects data and evidence to define the problem to be solved. See Tool 3.1: Framing a Problem of Practice for in-depth information and a template for conducting processes to identify and frame an actionable problem of practice.

In one school, for example, a principal and her teams see that student performance data is inconsistent across grade levels. Some classes or teams seem to be

Managing the change process

"The pessimist complains about the wind; the optimist expects it to change; the realist adjusts the sails," wrote author and educator William Arthur Ward. Change is all about adjusting the sails, no matter your circumstances. But it is how leaders manage and accelerate that change toward student achievement that will lead to the development of students and educators who are lifelong learners.

I believe in the theory of action illustrated in *Becoming a Learning System* (Learning Forward, 2018, p. 37). When we change educator knowledge, skills, and attitudes, we then change practice, which can lead to changes in student results. If educators are expected to change their beliefs about what and how students learn, they must work in an environment that promotes teamwork, vulnerability, and trust among the adults. They must be able to make mistakes and take risks, as long as any risk is based on what is best for students.

Each school year I repeat a very simple phrase to colleagues: "If adults like where they work, and are inspired by their colleagues, job challenges, and students, they will work harder and produce better quality work." I believe that to lead a school through the change process, the principal, as an instructional leader, creates the conditions needed to foster lasting change. And I have found that the most important elements conducive to change are the adult and student cultures. Yet fostering a positive adult culture, which then drives the student culture, was one of the tallest tasks that I tackled when I became principal at Fairfield Elementary eight years ago. The staff operated from a compliance mindset, there was little trust between teachers and administration, and fear had been used as a mechanism for change.

Early in my principal career I had been influenced by an article by Rick Torbin in which he wrote: "Organizational culture eats strategy for breakfast, lunch, and dinner." So, I took several steps to help build a more positive adult culture, including facilitating more

Principal Lindsay Amstutz-Martin (foreground) and colleagues take a break from planning.

frequent and authentic adult conversations about teaching and learning, building teaching teams and developing trusting relationships, creating opportunities for shared decision making, and convening ongoing staff appreciation efforts.

Moving from a just-tell-me-what-to-do environment into one that gives them the ability to decide and provide influence often proves challenging for adults. And that was the case at Fairfield through the first few years. Some staff members struggled with the autonomy they were given to make decisions. Yet, by continuing to leverage that agency to create and own a shared vision of what we want at Fairfield for our students, adults, and community, we have been able to change mindsets, adult practices, and student results.

Change is hard. As a former history teacher I frequently look to ancient philosophers for inspiration. Socrates said, "The secret of change is to focus all of your energy, not on fighting the old, but on building the new." The key to this process is deciding how to spend our energy and it is then that we will make changes that create the results we want in our schools.

— *Lindsay Amstutz-Martin*

CHAPTER 3

doing fine while others are struggling. One might begin with an assessment instrument such as a self-assessment aligned with the Professional Standards for Educational Leaders (PSEL). The data show weakness among leadership team members, particularly in Standard 4: Curriculum, Instruction, and Assessment. As a result of this lack of attention to curriculum, classroom observations show that rigorous instructional practices are not present in a majority of the classrooms in the school. A leader and her team may engage in the following series of "Why" questioning to home in on the root cause of the problem:

Q. Why are scores so inconsistent?
A. Some teachers have created excellent learning environments for their students while others struggle.

Q. Why are some teachers doing great while others struggle?
A. The school leadership hasn't created a support structure to share best practices and support those teachers (or teaching teams) that struggle.

Q. Why isn't the principal and school leadership team providing a system of support for teachers and teaching teams?
A. The leadership team doesn't have clarity on their role in supporting curriculum and instruction in the school.

In this example, the team has now zeroed in on a problem that they can frame in a problem statement and plan how they eventually will resolve it. A sample problem statement might read:

The principal and the school's leadership team lack clarity on their role in supporting curriculum and instruction in the school.

In all cases, clarifying problems to construct a problem statement is a complex process.

2. What is the potential solution or innovation? What research supports it?

The answer to the second question enables the principal and team to consider answers to the problem. Study and research regarding potential answers help provide a clearer picture of a desired solution. For example, a review of indicators for Standard 4 of the Professional Standards for Educational Leaders (NPBEA, 2015) will showcase the various types of behaviors required by the principal and team members. As a result of this exploration, the principal and the team produce a vision. In the case of the example started in Step 1, it might read as follows:

Example vision statement:
The principal and members of the building leadership team will (adapted from PSEL indicators):
1. Implement and support coherent systems of curriculum, instruction, and assessments that align to district and state guidelines.
2. Align and focus systems of curriculum, instruction, and assessments with and across grade levels to promote student academic success and well-being.
3. Ensure instructional practices are intellectually challenging, authentic to student experiences, recognize student strengths, and is differentiated to meet various learning needs.

As a result, teaching and learning will be more consistently rigorous and robust for all students.

3. What is the outcome sought? What will it look like when the desired results are achieved?

After establishing a clear vision of the solution to the problem, the principal and leadership team are

MANAGING CHANGE

SMART goals are:	
Strategic/ Specific	Focused on the precise needs of the learner.
Measurable	With information about how much of a change will be made and how educators will document the change.
Attainable	Realistically achieved given the resources and influence of the educators responsible.
Results oriented	Identifying specific outcomes that can be observed or measured.
Time bound	Specifying when the goal will be accomplished, with the timing appropriate to the scope of the goal.

Source: *Handbook for SMART School Teams: Revitalizing Best Practices for Collaboration,* Second edition, by Anne Conzemius and Jan O'Neill. Copyright 2013 Solution Tree Press.

now positioned to write a SMART goal (see sidebar, p. 37). In the current example, the goal might read something like:

> In six months, teachers across all grade levels will routinely facilitate college- and career-ready, standards-aligned rigorous learning in their classrooms using high-quality instructional materials.

4. What will staff and stakeholders need to learn and be able to do differently to achieve the desired results?

Answers to this question is another important component of the change plan. The KASAB acronym — Knowledge, Attitudes, Skills, Aspirations, Behaviors — is useful in guiding educators through the process of answering this question. Destin and the backwards bicycle (see p. 33) also give an example of the KASAB model in use. The model makes the point that knowledge is only part of the equation. Destin had the theoretical knowledge (K) about how to ride this particular bicycle. His goal was to change

his behavior (B) so that he could successfully ride it. In addition Destin had aspirations (A) to ride the bike and kept a positive attitude (A) throughout his eight-month learning journey. Those two components of the KASAB model are important when faculty and staffs engage in a long-term change process. As he began to practice, he utilized his skills (S) to put his knowledge to use. As a result, he developed a practice routine that led to his being able to ride the backwards bike.

The principal and leadership team in this example might develop the KASAB on page 38 (see Table 3.1: Understanding how KASAB Drives Educator Learning).

5. How will people acquire the new knowledge and skills?

At this stage in the process, the principal and leadership team have a more detailed picture of the changes they will support. They have clarified how success will look and what behaviors they expect from themselves, other educators, and stakeholders. The focus now shifts to "How do we get there?" Developing a clear theory of change proposes the best understanding of the relationships among our assumptions, strategies, outcomes, and results based on the date we collected to frame our problem. Developing this theory is helpful in informing a change management plan that will successfully support desired outcomes. Combined with the logic model, an action-planning tool, the theory of change guides the principal and leadership

Table 3.1: Understanding how KASAB Drives Educator Learning

KASAB	Descriptors
Knowledge	• Know what student standards have been adopted by the state or jurisdiction that inform teaching and learning throughout the school. • Clearly see the connections among leadership, curriculum, instructional materials, professional learning, and student outcomes. • Understand what makes curriculum resources and instructional materials high quality.
Attitudes	• Deeply believe that effective educational leaders develop and support intellectually rigorous and coherent systems of curriculum, instruction, and assessment to promote each student's academic success and well-being (Standard 4, PSEL). • Trust that the staff is willing to engage in a cycle of continuous improvement in order to strengthen their practice. • Believe that professional learning and systems of support will help teachers strengthen their practice.
Skills	• Provide the professional learning and structure to help teaching teams see connections among curriculum, instructional materials, professional learning, and student outcomes. • Skillfully facilitate learning teams through a cycle of continuous improvement. • Engage teaching teams in coaching and feedback conversations to inspire teachers and teaching teams to increase their effectiveness and improve their impact on student outcomes.
Aspirations	• Develop within the leadership team an internal desire to be seen by school staff as leaders of learning. • Create an atmosphere throughout the school that thrives on continuous improvement and results for each and every child.
Behaviors	• Communicate rigorous student learning expectations, assessment information, and instructional practices to teachers and students. • Provide actionable feedback to teachers that improves implementation of curriculum, assessment, and evidence-based instructional practices aligned to an integrated, tiered "system of supports" that meets the diverse needs of student learners. • Implement a formative assessment process to adjust ongoing teaching and learning to improve students' achievement of intended instructional outcomes (e.g., growth targets).

Source: Adapted with permission from *Professional Standards for Educational Leaders Rubric*, p. 10. Copyright 2019 Maryland State Department of Education.

MANAGING CHANGE

team as they seek to respond to these questions:
- What is the outcome sought? What will it look like when the desired results are achieved?
- What will staff and stakeholders need to learn and be able to do differently to achieve the desired results?
- How will people acquire the new knowledge and skills?

The theory of change articulates assumptions that undergird the actions chosen to support individual and organizational progress toward the vision and outcomes (see Tool 3.2: Developing a Theory of Change). As the principal and leadership team in the current example consider how they will move from current state to desired state, they might develop the following theory of change:
- If the principal and members of the leadership team engage in deep professional learning centered on the Professional Standards for Educational Leaders (PSEL), particularly Standard 4;
- And if the team also explores and unpacks the college- and career-ready standards adopted by their state and understands which are relevant for teachers in their building;
- And if the team creates a system of professional learning that engages staff in a cycle of continuous improvement;
- Then teachers learn to work in teaching teams to analyze data, set goals, learn individually and collaboratively, implement new learning, and monitor, assess, and adjust practice;
- So that, teachers at all grade levels will more consistently facilitate rigorous instruction using high-quality instructional materials; and
- Student performance will increase.

Visually, this theory of change would be depicted as follows in Figure 3.1.

Figure 3.1: Theory of Change

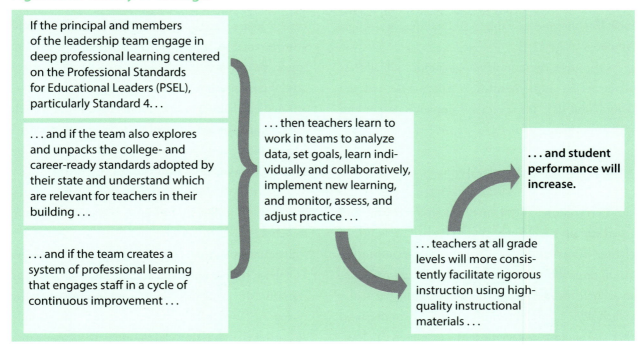

6. How will progress be monitored and follow-through provided to ensure success? How will effectiveness be measured?

The theory of change proposes a structure of how to move from a current to desired state, with an identification of all conditions required to achieve long-term outcomes. The logic model provides a comprehensive plan of action. A logic model details short-term, intermediate, and long-term outcomes and actions required to realize the vision. Logic models also identify the resources that will be needed as well as the person or people responsible for moving the work forward. A strong logic model has a series of assessment strategies to ensure all outcomes are measured (Kellogg Foundation, 2004). A logic model will provide the leadership team with a structure to answer the final questions (see Tool 3.3: Writing a Logic Model for further background and support).

Continuing with the example of the principal and leadership team seeking to strengthen their instructional leadership practice, a logic model may look like the one in Table 3.2: Example of a Logic Model on page 41.

Of course, the complete logic model will address all facets of implementation driving toward the completion date for successful implementation and goal attainment.

The role of stakeholders

Everyone has been involved in successful and failed attempts at change. Typical reasons for failure of change efforts can include lack of clarity regarding the vision or goal for the initiative, insufficient resources to achieve the change, or resistance from a particular stakeholder group. Learning principals understand that stakeholder engagement is not merely "telling" but instead involves listening, hearing, and honoring opinions of others. Absent support of the people being asked to make the change as well as those asked to endorse it, change efforts can be doomed to failure. Learning principals make stakeholder engagement a priority and understand the reasons for it.

Spiro (2011) writes that "Regardless of how good a change strategy is, there are groups benefiting from the status quo and therefore may feel threatened, angry, or disempowered if things change" (p. 53). She continues:

> Therefore, leading change effectively means accomplishing your goals in spite of opposition. So, it is important for leaders to recognize which groups might lose power or influence with the proposed changes, minimize their opposition, provide…for them to participate…but also plan for opposition that cannot be addressed. This is another way to say that you must address the politics inherent in leading any change strategy. (p. 53)

Schools serve an array of stakeholders who have varying interests and investments in the school's success. Primary stakeholders include the staff, central administration, and parents. Depending on the innovation, other stakeholders may include after-school program providers and caregivers who can be affected by changes to the school schedule. Textbook sales companies are affected when there are curriculum changes, and local businesses can be affected by families who act as consumers and employees.

Change is deeply personal. To understand stakeholders' different concerns, principals may use stakeholder assessments to identify the interests of key individuals and groups affected by a proposed change. For those people most affected by a new program or initiative the principal might begin by answering the question, "What's in it for me?" Leaders who are able to answer that question clearly and with a compelling

MANAGING CHANGE

Table 3.2: Example of a Logic Model

Long-term outcomes (8–12 months out)	Intermediate outcomes (6–7 months out)	Short-term outcomes (1–2 months out)	Resources available and other inputs	Person/people responsible
• Teachers at all grade levels will more consistently facilitate rigorous instruction using high-quality instructional materials. • Student performance increases.	• Leadership team creates a system of professional learning that engages staff in a cycle of continuous improvement where teaching teams analyze data, set goals, learn individually and collaboratively, implement new learning, and monitor, assess, and adjust practice.	• Principal and members of the leadership team engage in deep professional learning centered on the Professional Standards for Educational Leaders (PSEL), particularly Standard 4. • Team unpacks the college and career ready standards adopted by their state and understand, which are relevant for teachers in their building.	• Professional Standards for Educational Leaders • State college and career-ready standards • Standards for Professional Learning	• Principal • Members of the building leadership team • Cadre of instructional coaches
Assessment questions and measures	**Assessment questions and measures**	**Assessment questions and measures**		
• To what degree do teachers use high-quality instructional materials to consistently facilitate rigorous instruction aligned to state college- and career-ready standards (as measured by classroom observations, coaches' reports, and teachers' self-analyses)? • To what degree are students demonstrating proficiency across grade levels and subject areas (as measured by formative and summative assessments)?	• To what degree have professional learning systems been strengthened and aligned to a cycle of continuous improvement model (as evidenced by the principal's, leadership team's, and instructional coaches' observations)?	• To what degree has the team internalized the PSEL Standards (as measured by a self-assessment aligned to PSEL)? • To what extent has the team determined which curriculum standards are relevant (as evidenced by their ability to name the appropriate standards for grade levels and subject areas)?		

CHAPTER 3

rationale hold the key to launching and building support for a successful change effort.

There may still be those stakeholders, however, who prefer the status quo. Delineating each stakeholder group with investments in the status quo and answering the self-interest question for them is a valuable use of time. While the staff may represent one stakeholder group, specific answers may differ depending on a number of ways that staff members can be organized by the groups they represent (e.g. career stages, roles, assignments, or professional affiliations). Change-minded leaders utilize other strategies to build support and develop understanding of the need for change.

Authentically engaging with stakeholders is an important strategy to winning their support. By knowing the school's stakeholders, the learning principal can engage intentionally with diverse perspectives and begin to build relationships before considering specific innovations or programs. Respectful relationships grounded in shared learning experiences and discussions of differing perspectives can lead to respect and trust that contribute to crafting a change agenda with most stakeholders behind it. There always will be stakeholders who may not be required to make dramatic changes but whose support is necessary for the change to happen. A new school schedule, for example, may require support from the school district and bus drivers. A change to the professional learning priorities may require consent from the Chief Academic Officer. As a result, school leaders consider stakeholders whose support may be needed at some point in the process and plan how they can be informed, consulted, and engaged. Establishing a plan to assess their readiness for support and engagement in the process is also important to the work. Having a plan for monitoring and sustaining commitment is equally important.

Taking action

Principals and assistant principals routinely manage fiscal, human, and physical resources to provide excellent teaching and learning. Of the many management challenges facing school leaders, guiding school staff members through the process of planning and implementing change is one of the most complex. Change management is difficult because it is a dynamic process affected by multiple forces and many actors. Learning principals recognize that knowledge is insufficient without the skills and tools to manage change successfully. Learning principals invest deeply in building expertise in all areas.

Principals can take the following actions help them and their staffs understand change, take intentional actions, and measure their progress toward intended results:

1. Assess and establish leader readiness for change

The previous discussion on readiness focused on the individuals and institutions required to change within a plan for improvement. However, the readiness of the principal to undertake any change effort is equally, if not more, important. Jody Spiro (2011) presents three tools that address the readiness of the leader, the staff or participants, and the school. The leader's readiness rubric asks questions such as the following:

Experience: To what degree do you have previous experience with change in general and with this type of change in particular?

1. Have you successfully led change in any organization before, especially an organization similar to the current one?

42 The LEARNING PRINCIPAL

Learning Forward

2. Have you successfully led change in this organization before?

3. Have you led change in any organization unsuccessfully?

4. Do you have previous successful experience in the technical content area of the change strategy?

5. Have you been able to "unfreeze" participants' previously negative experiences with change and motivate them to take a leap of faith now? (p. 31)

Whatever it takes: To what degree are you willing to do whatever it takes?

1. Do you have competing priorities that might demand your attention and detract from your leadership of the change strategy?

2. Are you reluctant to label a group as "low readiness?" Are you reluctant to put a lot of structure into your planning and implementation processes?

3. Do you believe that you should always treat everyone equally as colleagues regardless of their readiness to participate in the change strategy?

4. Do you consult people whose views may differ from your own?

5. Are you open to the resulting plan being different from your original conception (provided that the nonnegotiable conditions are in there)?

Answering these questions can help principals identify their current strengths and areas for growth in facilitating change. Principals can use the results to identify a personal learning plan to develop their knowledge and skills in managing change. Learn more by reading *Leading Change Handbook: Concepts and Tools* (Spiro, 2018) and using the readiness rubric (pp. 3–6).

2. Focus on individuals as well as organizational structures

Stages of Concern
6: Refocusing
5: Collaboration
4: Consequence
3: Management
2: Personal
1: Informational
0: Unconcerned

As mentioned earlier in the chapter, change is deeply personal and principals can benefit from specific tools to use with individuals immersed in it. Shirley Hord and Gene Hall (2015) are the lead architects of a change model and set of diagnostic tools that educators use to facilitate change. The Concerns-Based Adoption Model contains dimensions that leaders use to measure different aspects of individual educators' concerns throughout the implementation of any change. Principals may use the Stages of Concern Questionnaire (SoCQ) to organize educators' different feelings into defined Stages of Concern.

When a new initiative or major change occurs in a school, educators often begin at Stage 0: Unconcerned. They know an innovation, or change, is being considered or has been introduced, but they are not yet interested. Over time, and with guidance from the leader, they move into Stage 1: Informational. Here, they are beginning to express some interest about the change. At this point, they show no commitment to engaging in the change, but they are interested in learning more. At Stage 2: Personal, teachers and other staff members want to know how they will be personally affected by change. They ask, "What does this change mean for the way I teach?" At Stage 3: Management, teachers begin to think about how they will manage the change in practice. At this level, they are starting to consider the technical consequences of the change and how it may impact their routines. At Stage 4: Consequence, teachers begin to consider the impact of the change on others. They begin to ask questions like, "How might this change affect my students?"

As teachers reach the final two stages, they begin to work through implementation of the change. At Stage 5: Collaboration, teachers begin to consider working with colleagues in order to make the change effective. Finally, at Stage 6: Refocusing, teachers innovate and refine the new strategy in order to better meet the needs of their students or the situation. At this point, they often fully accept and understand the change.

The SoCQ supports principals in identifying individual's stages of concerns and appropriate supports to address them. The principal, acting as the leader of learning, creates the conditions to help teachers progress through the Stages of Concern and build capacity to move the change forward. An example innovation is a new set of guidelines for student discipline that has been adopted by the district. Initially, teachers may not be interested in or are resistant to the changes. For example, "I heard about them, but those new guidelines don't really apply to us," some staff might argue. Effective leaders provide staff with multiple opportunities to engage with the new information. They provide research findings to support the new guidelines and they give teams of teachers opportunities to dig deeper into the impending change. Because change is about learning and is also a social enterprise, these structured learning opportunities will help teachers work through their stages of concern and ultimately move to full use of a new practice. See Tool 3.4: Using the Concerns-based Adoption Model and Stages of Concern for additional help in introducing the Stages of Concern.

A related but different dimension is the Levels of Use (LoU). While Stages of Concern focus on educator's attitudes, feelings, and perceptions related to a change initiative, the LoU focuses on the behaviors of teachers and staff members relative to the change, specifically, changes in their practices. The concept of levels of use, therefore, applies to groups and entire institutions as education leaders assess "the degree and fidelity with which staff are using the program" (AIR, 2020, para. 1).

Levels of Use:	
(0)	Nonuse
(I)	Orientation
(II)	Preparation
(III)	Mechanical Use
(IVA)	Routine
(IVB)	Refinement
(V)	Integration
(VI)	Renewal

The LoU interview protocols organize actual innovations that individuals undertake into categories spanning Nonuse to Renewal (see sidebar). Through a facilitated series of interviews with staff members, principals can measure changes in practice as well as the extent to which staff are effectively implementing a new program and where they may need additional support. See "Levels of Use: Concerns-Based Adoption Model" (https://www.air.org/resource/levels-use-concerns-based-adoption-model) for guidance and resources about this CBAM dimension and others.

3. Engage stakeholders

Recognizing that stakeholders will be key to the success of any change initiative, learning principals create structures to ensure that all stakeholders are represented appropriately in decision making and planning structures. For example, schools may have leadership councils, principal advisory groups, grade-level or subject-based learning teams, faculty advisory groups, parent organizations, community councils, and more. Learning principals may consider four key steps to engaging stakeholders and building the trust and support essential for launching and sustaining change efforts:

MANAGING CHANGE

1. Learning principals ensure diversity of experience, race, gender, ethnicity, and perspectives in all representative bodies;

2. They prioritize shared learning experiences as part of each agenda;

3. Learning principals engage stakeholders in examining data and other information that builds a case for change; and

4. Finally, learning principals enlist these stakeholders in planning for and understanding the change process.

4. Celebrate early wins

In the book *Becoming a Learning System* (2018), the authors emphasized the importance of celebrating progress. They stated that celebrations reignite the human spirit and propel staff toward even greater accomplishments. Celebrations can touch hearts and fire imaginations, bonding people together and connecting them to the organization's goals, vision, and values.

As leaders successfully support their staff through the change process, they need to celebrate their accomplishments along the way. As emphasized throughout this chapter, change is challenging and often accompanied by what Michael Fullan (2001) coined the "implementation dip," or that time when things become more confusing and challenging before success is achieved. Taking time to celebrate "early wins" reinforces that the school is on the right path and creates energy and momentum to sustain effort through the most challenging parts of the process.

Spiro (2011) suggests that

an effective change leader deliberately plans for small, early wins that demonstrate concretely that achieving the change goal is feasible and will result in benefits for those involved…

You should plan for achieving and documenting important results that are evident within the first month or two. Of course, all involved must agree that achieving this "win" would result in something positive — that is, meeting a common definition of "success" — and further the overall change strategy. By doing so, you will inspire confidence that the rest of the initiative can be accomplished. (p. 91)

See Tool 3.5: Establishing and Celebrating Early Wins for guidance in developing this process.

Conclusion

Much has been written about how to support staff through the change process. Michael Fullan (2005) described eight forces influencing the leadership of change. He argues there are specific leadership actions that create effective and lasting change. He writes that when staff understand the process, they can more effectively engage in it. He contends that focusing on leadership for change involves thinking through who leads various aspects of the change, and what traits will they require to be successful. It assumes that change doesn't happen without the engagement of effective leaders throughout the process.

Fullan's message is clear: Leaders play a special role in supporting staff through the change process. Like Hord and Roussin (2013), Fullan believes change is a learning process. Engaging staff members in a series of learning experiences and collaborative exchanges greatly increases the likelihood they will successfully accomplish any major change. The learning principal uses the knowledge and tools to facilitate a process that taps the individual and collective passion, perspective, and commitment of the entire school community to achieve the vision it has for its students.

CHAPTER 3

Reflections

- What more do I want to learn about change theories and processes and how will I go about learning it?

- What are potential benefits from assessing readiness of myself and my entire school community?

- What new planning approaches and tools will I apply to my change efforts?

- How will I engage stakeholders in the future to improve change efforts?

- How could planning for early wins support our school improvement agenda?

References

AIR. (2020). *Levels of Use: Concerns-Based Adoption Model.* [Website]. Available at https://www.air.org/resource/levels-use-concerns-based-adoption-model

Conzemius, A. & O'Neill, J. (2013). *Handbook for SMART school teams: Revitalizing best practices for collaboration* (2nd ed.). Solution Tree Press.

Fullan, M. (2005). 8 forces for leaders of change. *JSD, 26*(4), 54–64.

Fullan, M. (2001). *The new meaning of educational change* (3rd ed.). Teachers College Press.

Heifetz, R. & Linsky, M. (2002). *Leadership on the line: Staying alive through the dangers of change.* Harvard Business School Press.

Hirsh, S. & Crow, T. (2018). *Becoming a learning team: A guide to a teacher-led cycle of continuous improvement* (2nd ed.). Learning Forward.

Hirsh, S., Psencik, K., & Brown, F. (2018). *Becoming a learning system* (Revised ed.). Learning Forward.

Hord, S. & Hall, G. (2015). *Implementing change: Patterns, principles, and potholes* (4th ed.). Pearson.

Hord, S. & Roussin, J. (2013). *Implementing change through learning: Concerns-based concepts, tools, and strategies for guiding change.* Corwin.

Leithwood, K., Seashore-Louis, K., Anderson, S., & Wahlstrom, K. (2004). *How leadership influences student learning.* The Wallace Foundation.

Maryland State Department of Education. (2018, July). *Professional Standards for Educational Leaders rubric.* Maryland State Department of Education (MSDE) and Community Training and Assistance Center (CTAC).

National Policy Board for Educational Administration (2015). *Professional Standards for Educational Leaders.* Author.

Smarter Every Day. (2015, April 24). The backwards brain bicycle #133. Available at https://www.youtube.com/watch?v=MFzDaBzBlL0

Spiro, J. (2011). *Leading change step-by-step: Tactics, tools, and tales.* Jossey-Bass.

Spiro, J. (2018). *Leading change handbook: Concepts and tools.* Available at The Wallace Foundation Knowledge Center at https://www.wallacefoundation.org/knowledge-center/Documents/leading-change-handbook.pdf

W.K. Kellogg Foundation. (2004, January). *Using logic models to bring together planning, evaluation, and action: Logic model development guide.* Author. Available at https://www.wkkf.org/resource-directory/resources/2004/01/logic-model-development-guide

Tools index for Chapter 3

Tool	Title	Use
3.1	Framing a Problem of Practice	This tool is useful in determining and articulating the root causes of problems that affect teaching and learning at a school.
3.2	Developing a Theory of Change	This tool provides a framework for developing an actionable theory of change that includes both learning goals and potential barriers to achievement of those goals.
3.3	Writing a Logic Model	This tool, a complement to Tool 3.2, is a framework for describing expectations for change relative to outcomes, resources, responsibilities, and time frame.
3.4	Using the Concerns-based Adoption Model and Stages of Concern	This tool offers direction to resources about specific diagnostic tools to understand the change process and how to support staff members who are changing their practices.
3.5	Establishing and Celebrating Early Wins	This tool offers a resource for developing a strategy to achieve short-term successes that lead to long-term change.

CHAPTER
4

Designing learning

Where are we now?

The principal understands adult learning theories and how to apply them in designing professional learning.

STRONGLY AGREE | AGREE | NO OPINION | DISAGREE | STRONGLY DISAGREE

The principal focuses on equitable outcomes for all students as a driver for professional learning.

STRONGLY AGREE | AGREE | NO OPINION | DISAGREE | STRONGLY DISAGREE

The principal clearly connects designs for professional learning to intended educator and student data and outcomes.

STRONGLY AGREE | AGREE | NO OPINION | DISAGREE | STRONGLY DISAGREE

The principal builds coherent and aligned learning agendas for individuals, teams, and entire faculty.

STRONGLY AGREE | AGREE | NO OPINION | DISAGREE | STRONGLY DISAGREE

The principal creates structures and processes to support implementation of an effective and purposeful learning agenda.

STRONGLY AGREE | AGREE | NO OPINION | DISAGREE | STRONGLY DISAGREE

The principal attends to individual choice and voice in the school learning plan.

STRONGLY AGREE | AGREE | NO OPINION | DISAGREE | STRONGLY DISAGREE

CHAPTER 4

A learning principal takes risks and pushes the desire for new knowledge and improved practices in herself as well as in collaboration with colleagues. Building trusting relationships with all staff members is critical if such collaborative learning is to occur. A learning principal implements and refines new learning to encourage growth in teachers' educational practices and, ultimately, to make a positive impact on student learning. A learning principal is inspired to build enthusiasm with teams of educators by celebrating successes and sharing how she has observed and implemented practice that transforms learning in others.

Carrie Kennedy
Principal, Fred H. Croninger Elementary School
Fort Wayne Community Schools
Fort Wayne, Indiana

Overview

In a learning school, everyone involved shares an understanding of the role professional learning plays in advancing school purposes, their responsibilities for professional learning, and the time and resources required. Those who work in such a school experience a culture of continuous learning.

The principals who create and lead the staff members of learning schools build effective, results-oriented learning agendas that are grounded in powerful designs for professional learning. Recognizing a substantial knowing-doing gap between what educators know and what happens in classrooms, learning principals commit to leveraging the very best theories, research, and models of human learning to close that gap. They maintain an intense focus on the goals of the school, the teams, and most importantly the individual learners. They take into account their adult learners' various characteristics, their comfort with the learning process and one another, their familiarity with the content, the magnitude of the expected change, the work environment, and resources available to support learning. Of prime importance is connecting what adults need to learn to what students are expected to know and do well.

Learning Forward promotes standards-based professional learning as fundamental to changing educators' knowledge, skills, and dispositions, which, in turn, support changes in educator practice to support improvement in student outcomes (see Chapter 3: Managing Change). These actions and their outcomes appear deceptively simple but require sophisticated planning and implementation, as well as continuous assessment.

The first three chapters of this book describe how the learning principal establishes essential conditions and applies the change process to achieve a high-performing school. Learning principals know that the right conditions, equity-focused staff members, and high-quality instructional materials are foundational components of success. Substantive improvements require attention to the change process and logic model that describes the adult learning essential to achieve ambitious goals for students. Throughout the change process, educators set goals at the school, team, and individual levels for different purposes. The Learning Designs standard supports this complex process: "Professional learning that increases educator effectiveness and results for all students integrates theories, research, and models of human learning to achieve its intended outcomes" (Learning Forward, 2011, p. 40).

The adult learner

In 1968 Malcolm Shepherd Knowles (1984) introduced the term andragogy and offered principles that distinguish adult from student learners. When school leaders design learning for their staff members, they apply the principles acknowledging that adult learners have knowledge and skills that contribute to the planning process; they have more life experiences upon which to build; and they are typically more motivated by intrinsic rewards than extrinsic.

Judy Arin Krupp (1987) introduced the theory that educators' stage in life affects their propensity toward learning. Different life stages (e.g. early career, early marriage, parenthood, empty nester) as well as ages influence adults' interests, commitments to career, professional growth priorities, and more. Principals can use this information as another guide for understanding staff members' behaviors and inform choices among learning designs. Some principals are familiar with Anthony Gregorc (1984) and others who advance instruments that enable adults to gain deeper perspectives on their own preferred learning

Being fully invested in the teaching and learning process is the foundation for being a learning principal. Teaching and learning must be the number-one priority each and every day. It is the key to student success because a focus on learning puts kids first! The principal, as the lead learner, learns with other principals how to set growth goals and collaborate within their own communities of practice to set the stage for effective, high-quality instruction. Within her own school, the learning principal does not make decisions in isolation, but instead, joins teams of teachers to support one another in completing the cycle of continuous improvement.

Destini Martin
Principal, William F. Barnett Elementary
Santa Fe ISD
Santa Fe, Texas

CHAPTER 4

Using learning designs to succeed
Teams push through the cycle of continuous improvement

With development of new state math standards, the staff at Dan J. Kubacak Elementary struggled with implementation. Members of the leadership team observed that teachers were not fully engaging students in their work. Math teams, for example, were challenged to understand the depth of the standards, so teachers were unable to apply resources effectively or align assessments correctly with instruction and the standards. They also were using assessments after a lengthy period of time; consequently, students had limited retention of concepts. Teachers were unable to reteach effectively to increase student success in achieving priority standards.

Our first action was to implement the guided math workshop model focusing on small-group instruction to give students the skills they would need to meet new standards. We knew that professional learning would be the key to helping teachers shift from our traditional ways of teaching math to the math workshop. We also included the instructional coaching model. By using KASAB protocols and a short cycle of continuous improvement within professional learning communities, teachers were able to refine their instruction through focused, results-driven coaching cycles. This job-embedded learning design gave teams a way to learn and grow with one another.

The next step was to think differently about how we planned within teacher teams. We needed to make sure each team member could understand the standards for each unit, analyze available resources, and select the most relevant so they could implement accurate, rigorous math lessons and units for our students. We had discussed the idea of backward design and "planning with the end in mind" on several different occasions; we knew it was time to put it into action. Although teams struggled through the process, principals and coaches worked closely with them to complete planning for each unit. We immediately found that standards were being taught incorrectly, and as a result, resources, instruction, and assessment were misaligned. The math instructional coach stated, "It was amazing to watch our teams develop their own understanding of standards and how instructional practices, resources, and assessments work together to enhance student achievement."

Teams also began to use short cycles of continuous improvement within each unit. Team members planned units by building formative goals based on historical data and priority standards. They developed common assessments, designed lessons, and vetted resources they would use in teaching the units. After they completed units they analyzed data from

Principal Destini Martin (center right, seated) and teacher team review learning plans.

DESIGNING LEARNING

the formative unit assessments. Then, they created a reteach/reassess goal to move into second-order change and complete the cycle of continuous improvement. Teaching teams knew that they would have to analyze a standard differently when they were reteaching it, and so they started the cycle once again with the priority standard (see Example learning design framework).

At the end of the year's learning cycles, we had applied research-based programming, standards analysis, common-assessment building, and focused coaching cycles. We had executed precise planning, vetted our resources, and completed short cycles of continuous improvement. That combination of learning designs and strategies yielded high results for Kubacak Elementary students. The 5th-grade math students made high gains in their cohorts, thus closing their achievement gap. Reports of state assessment scores indicated a 14% gain in "Approaches [the standard]," 19% gain in "Meets [the standard]," and 16% gain in "Masters [the standard]." The campus also received three distinctions for outstanding achievement from the state of Texas and went from 73 to 86 in overall performance.

— *Destini Martin*

Example learning design framework to address the Texas Essential Knowledge and Skills (TEKS)

Team leader:
Team members in attendance:
Summative SMART Goal:
Norms:
Unit and Priority TEKS:
What is our common assessment data telling us for this unit? What are our priority TEKS?
What do we want students to learn?
What are the common misconceptions?
What is our formative SMART goal for this unit based on historical data and priority standards?
What is our professional learning goal for this unit? KASAB K: What do we need to know? A: What attitude do we need to have? S: What skills do we need to have, learn, refine? A: What are our aspirations? B: What behaviors do we want to see in teachers and students?
How is our implementation plan working?
How are our strategies working for students who have not attained proficiency?
How are our strategies working for students who have attained proficiency?
Best practices that were shared during the meeting:
Implementation learning design: (Lesson Study, Student Work Analysis, Tuning Protocol)
What strategies are we utilizing for our reassessed/retaught TEK?
What evidence do we have that our plan is working? Attach data digs and action plans
What is our retaught/reassessed TEK for this unit? What is our reassessed SMART goal? What unit will we include this reassessed TEK?

CHAPTER 4

styles. Principals may use these instruments to provide information that guides selection of learning designs that meet individuals' strengths and more.

Bruce Joyce and his co-authors have long campaigned to end one-shot training experiences for educators. In partnerships with local school systems to implement the practices described in his book *Models of Teaching* (2015) now in its 9th edition, he discovered the importance of practice and coaching to launch and sustain change in teacher performance. His research with Beverly Showers established definitively the importance of follow-up and support in professional learning, including coaching (see Table 4.1: Effectiveness of Professional Learning Elements).

Table 4.1 also underscores the need for educator learning that takes into account each of the aspects, Knowledge, Attitudes, Skills, Aspirations, and Behaviors (KASAB) examined in Chapter 3. The end goal of applying KASAB is not gaining knowledge; it is changing practice to impact student learning. School leaders serious about implementing substantive change in classrooms prioritize and invest in the long-term support that would be required to realize their vision of a culture of continuous learning.

Jane Vella in *Learning to Listen, Learning to Teach: The Power of Dialogue in Educating Adults* (1994),

offers a comprehensive description of adult learning preferences. In addition to concepts introduced earlier, she addresses the context and setting for learning including key ideas of safe spaces for learning, opportunities to build relationships, and facilitating learning with others. These 12 principles (see sidebar, p. 55), as well as the research and theories that preceded and informed them, offer powerful insights for principals committed to establishing a learning culture and leveraging learning designs that will achieve their intended outcomes. These principles are represented in the actions that principals take as lead learning designers.

Adult learning models and designs

As learning principals apply their understanding of effective adult learning to the design of what educators will experience, Learning Forward's (2011) Learning Designs standard elevates important components of adult learning models and designs:

Learning designs that engage adult learners in applying the processes they are expected to use facilitate the learning of those behaviors by making them more explicit. Effective

Table 4.1: Effectiveness of Professional Learning Elements

Components	Knowledge	Skill	Transfer
	Learners understand the content	Learners demonstrate they can use the practices	Learners implement practice in the classroom
Study of theory	10%	5%	0%
Demonstration	30%	20%	0%
Practice	60%	60%	5%
Peer coaching	95%	95%	99%

Source: *Student achievement through staff development* (3rd ed.) by Bruce Joyce and Beverly Showers. Copyright 2002 Association for Supervision and Curriculum Development.

DESIGNING LEARNING

Twelve Principles of Adult Learning

Principle	Description	Action
1. Needs assessment	Informs the course.	Listening to learners' wants and needs helps to shape professional learning that has immediate usefulness to adults.
2. Safety	Creating a safe environment for learning.	Create an inviting setting for learners. Begin with simple, clear, and easy tasks before advancing to more complex or difficult ones. The environment is nonjudgmental.
3. Sound relationships	The power of friendship and respect.	Foster an open communication process involving respect, safety, and listening. Balance between advocacy and inquiry. Relationships must transcend personal likes and dislikes.
4. Sequence and reinforcements	Knowing where and how to begin.	Organize session knowledge, skills, and attitudes in an order that goes from easy to complex and from group-supported to solo efforts.
5. Praxis (Practice)	Action with reflection.	Doing with built-in reflection and ongoing beautiful dance of inductive and deductive forms of learning. Doing–reflecting–deciding–changing–new doing.
6. Respect for learners	Recognizing learners are decision makers.	The dialogue of learning is between subjects, not objects. Learners suggest and make decisions about what occurs in the learning event.
7. Ideas, feelings, and actions	Cognitive, affective, and psychomotor.	Conceptualize it, get a chance to feel it, and do something with it.
8. Immediacy	Perception evokes reality.	Learners experience the immediate usefulness and relevance of new learning, what makes a difference now. Combine with sequence and reinforcement.
9. Clear roles and role development	The death of the "professor."	Whatever impedes dialogue must be courageously addressed and eradicated. Whatever enables dialogue must be fearlessly nurtured and used.
10. Teamwork	Small-group learning teams.	Teams provide a quality of safety that is effective and helpful.
11. Engagement	Learning as an active process.	Invite learners to put themselves into the learning task.
12. Accountability	Success is in the eyes of the learner.	How do learners know they know?

Source: *Learning to Listen, Learning to Teach: The Power of Dialogue in Educating Adults* by Jane Vella, p. 4. Copyright 1994 Jossey-Bass.

CHAPTER 4

designs for professional learning assist educators in moving beyond comprehension of the surface features of a new idea or practice to developing a more complete understanding of its purposes, critical attributes, meaning, and connection to other approaches. To increase student learning, educator learning provides many opportunities for educators to practice new learning with ongoing assessment, feedback, and coaching so the learning becomes fully integrated into routine behaviors. (p. 41–42)

Sparks and Loucks-Horsley (1989) introduced the five models framework that included individually guided, observation/assessment, involvement in a development/ improvement process, training, and inquiry. Even today educators will recognize how their most familiar learning designs still fall within one of these five categories. And, while there is some reluctance to use the word training in the field, as part of this list it is possible to distinguish training from the other forms and approaches to learning.

Frameworks are helpful to understanding how to approach learning design. Lois Easton (2015)

Table 4.2: Framework of Learning Designs

Components	Elements
Environment	• Participants • Conditions
Delivery	• Structure • Accessibility • Aesthetics • Content • Features • Tools
Action	• Transference • Flexibility

Source: *Powerful Designs for Professional Learning,* Third Edition by Lois Brown Easton, p. 6. Copyright 2015 Learning Forward.

offered a framework designed to help decision makers recognize key differences among various learning designs and appropriate situations in which to use them. Each design was presented through the lens of three components: Environment, Delivery, Action (see Table 4.2: Framework of Learning Designs).

Environment components focus on needs, goals, learners, and setting for learning. Delivery components focus on clarity of adult learning outcomes (i.e. KASAB), pragmatic arrangements, participant engagement, modes of delivery, and materials and resources. Action addresses practice and reflection (Easton, 2015 pp. 5–6). Easton's intention was to ensure that decisions were guided by goals, context, processes, and most importantly, impact. Tool 4.1: Selecting a Learning Design will support decision making regarding learning designs for the school learning agenda.

In *Becoming a Learning System, Revised Edition,* Stephanie Hirsh, Kay Psencik, and Frederick Brown (2018) examined and ranked popular learning designs according to three elements within Easton's framework: degree to which the learning design shifts instructional practice, degree of trust, and level of complexity required to implement the design. This analysis gives learning principals a starting point from which to consider where to invest resources as they plan learning (see sidebar, p. 57).

Designing a learning agenda

To supplement the vision, mission, theory of action, and logic models that ground school improvement work, learning principals oversee the schoolwide professional learning plan. Hirsh, Psencik, and Brown (2018) describe this schoolwide professional learning plan as a learning agenda, which specifically "connects adult learning to essential student learning.

DESIGNING LEARNING

Analyzing Learning Designs	
Learning Design	**Characteristics**
• Lesson study • Analyzing student work • Tuning protocol • Videotaping and analyzing lessons	• Shifts practices over time • Requires high trust • Greater complexity
• Critical friends' groups • Peer observations • Action research	• Medium results in shifting practice • Medium level of trust required • Medium complexity
• Book studies • Classroom walk-throughs • Case studies • Online webinars	• Low yield in shifting practices • Low level of trust required • Easy to organize

Source: *Becoming a Learning System,* Revised Edition by Stephanie Hirsh, Kay Psencik, and Frederick Brown, p. 134. Copyright 2018 Learning Forward.

Designers plan adult learning only after identifying student needs…and the adults clearly understand the link between their learning and student learning" (p. 131).

Just as teachers are expected to offer students powerful lessons that attend to all elements essential to successful learning, learning principals consider all essential adult learning theories and research when developing the learning agenda for teachers. Learning principals use three key questions to guide the development of such a learning agenda: 1) What do students need to know and be able to do? 2) What do the educators need to know and be able to do to support student learning? 3) How will educators acquire the necessary knowledge, attitudes, skills, aspirations, and dispositions detailed in the answer to Question 2?

Problems often occur when schools respond to Question 1 by adopting new programs or committing to professional development without fully understanding the answers to Questions 2 and 3. To answer Questions 2 and 3, educators need not only a sophisticated understanding of student and educator data, standards, curriculum, instruction, and

assessment, but also a deep understanding of the various learning designs that are best situated to accelerate educator learning and practice toward the desired outcomes. See Tool 4.2: Designing a Learning Agenda for a template of a learning agenda.

In addition, the principal and other decision makers will need to answer the following questions:

- Which of the student needs must be addressed by all staff members?
- Which questions and answers are specific to certain grade levels or courses?
- Are there questions and answers that are specific to small groups of individuals (perhaps new teachers) or selected individuals?

Once learning principals address these questions, they can set priorities for schoolwide learning as well as grade- or subject-matter teams. With these priorities established, school leaders determine what learning is mandatory and what will be voluntary. Some needs are so great that everyone will need to participate; however, the learning designs literature suggests that while learning the content may be nonnegotiable, there may be options in how best to achieve the desired results.

CHAPTER 4

When learning principals and other school leaders have a deeper understanding of various learning designs, they are better positioned to design powerful learning experiences and advise or coach others as they make decisions about their personal learning agendas. School leaders understand that selecting the wrong designs will lead to disappointing results, wasted resources, and deplete trust in future endeavors. Few decisions are more important in determining the future trajectory of a school.

Once limited by time and access, educators today have a plethora of options for engaging in continuous learning. As a result, it is even more important that principals offer guidance for navigating various decision points. Learning principals recognize the importance of engaging staff in the selection and facilitation of learning designs. Learning principals ensure educators set clear goals at the school, team, and individual levels. As the Learning Designs standard states,

> Appropriate options for meeting agreed-upon goals attend to: backgrounds, experiences, beliefs, motivation, interests, cognitive processes, professional identity, and commitment. Decisions about learning designs consider all phases of the learning process, from knowledge and skill acquisition to application, reflection, refinement, assessment, and evaluation. Learning designers consider how to build knowledge, develop skills, transform practice, challenge attitudes and beliefs, and inspire action. (Learning Forward, 2011, p. 42)

Taking action

Learning principals integrate effective adult learning into the daily work of schools as a central element of creating a schoolwide environment of continuous improvement. In addition to making their own

learning as leaders visible, principals take the following actions to leverage professional learning as a core element of achieving equitable outcomes for all students.

1. Provide structures and support for continuous learning

"Education research shows that most school variables, considered separately, have at most small effects on learning. The real payoff comes when individual variables combine to reach critical mass. Creating the conditions under which that can occur is the job of the principal" (The Wallace Foundation, 2013, p. 4). Learning principals create the structures, procedures, frameworks, calendars, and schedules that are essential to standards-based professional learning. They establish multiple teams and explain the critical roles each takes to advance the school vision and goals as well as design and implement the learning agenda. They share this story through the words, actions, and visuals that help all stakeholders to understand and embrace it.

Multiple teams may include the school leadership team, grade-level or department-level teams, and specialty teams organized to address other school priorities. Structures help to clarify representation on various teams and the criteria for participation. Principals explain their understanding of the critical roles each team takes to advance the school vision and goals and invite everyone into the process of delineating roles and responsibilities. Providing clear criteria for leading and serving helps all staff members to recognize the importance of the roles and responsibilities they are asked to fulfill in creating a learning school.

Calendars and schedules offer visual demonstrations of the principal's commitment to the structures and procedures put in place for learning. Time is appropriately allocated for the various teams to meet their responsibilities. For example, effective learning teams are scheduled to meet three to four times per week for a minimum of three hours. School leadership teams may meet about two to three hours per month. And while state and local policies often make it difficult for school leaders to find such blocks of time, learning principals do not wait for policymakers to act; they find creative solutions to provide time for achieving school learning goals. As important as finding the time to learn, is using the time to learn. The learning principal models learning-focused uses of this time by transforming faculty meetings into learning sessions, data analysis sessions, or collaborative analyses of student work.

How principals choose to allocate their own time to support staff learning is one way they signal their priorities. Here are a few questions principals may consider when creating schedules for themselves and other key support personnel:

- How much time will they spend in classrooms supporting teacher growth?
- How much time will they spend with teams? Will there be a set schedule?
- How much time will coaches be expected to spend in direct support of teachers and/or learning teams?
- How will specialty area teachers and other support staff (e.g. counselors, social workers) have access to learning teams and other growth opportunities?

Time is a limited resource requiring principals to frequently make tough decisions. Learning principals ensure that their decisions align with school and team goals. While some decisions are not always popular, they are respected if clearly justified. Chapter 5 further discusses the issue of resource allocation.

2. Prioritize equity in planning professional learning

Learning principals understand the multifaceted relationship between achieving equity and professional learning. They take intentional actions that make it possible for professional learning to realize its full power as an equity lever.

First, only when all educators experience the opportunity to learn at high levels will all students experience the best teaching that a school has to offer, which is why learning principals are fierce guardians of teachers' collaborative use of the learning cycle, as explored in Chapter 1, as well as a full range of learning suited to their needs and goals.

Next, learning principals who prioritize equity realize when educators' knowledge, practices, and beliefs may benefit from an explicit focus on culturally responsive teaching. Such a focus might happen at the school level, yet a more sustained approach embedded in teachers' learning team goals and learning cycle may prove to be more beneficial. And, learning principals will hold themselves responsible for not only championing culturally responsive practices but also being expert in such practices themselves.

The focus on beliefs, which learning principals explore through their work as change leaders, is critical to achieving equity-driven growth. Learning principals will invite ongoing discussion and reflection about issues of systemic racism, unconscious bias, and the impact of beliefs on practice for themselves and their teams. Their goal is continually to strive to dismantle long-standing barriers to learning for students of color in particular. Such conversations may begin with literature studies (e.g. *Courageous Conversations About Race,* 2015; "Equity," *The Learning Professional,* October, 2018; *How to be an Antiracist,* 2019). Tool 4.3: Advancing Equity provides the background and ground rules for hosting such conversations.

Finally, learning principals' uses of data, and the ways they support teams to use data in goal setting, will continually identify how all groups of students are progressing. Learning principals will draw upon a wide range of data sources to explore not only achievement but also engagement, attendance, student input, and student work to unearth root causes. Principals and their teams will pinpoint for which students their efforts to improve fall short and make adjustments to change students' learning trajectories.

3. Use procedures and protocols to increase effectiveness

Selecting or establishing frameworks schoolwide to guide the work of each team promotes shared understandings and propels work forward. Instead of each team inventing how it will spend its time together, routine procedures and protocols allow team leaders to focus more on substance than process. Learning principals see consistent staff agreements and meeting norms as key to sustaining a learning culture. Making public such statements addresses two of the conditions essential to successful adult learning: create the safe and productive learning space and build relationships (Vella, 1994). Staff agreements delineate how staff interact with each other at all times — for example, "We show gratitude toward each other daily." Meeting norms add a layer of specificity about what takes place in meetings, for example, "Every meeting starts and ends on time." A small group can draft such agreements and then the entire faculty can discuss and revise to build understanding and consensus. Regularly reviewing staff agreements and meeting norms, discussing exemplars and nonexemplars of each, and reflecting on group and individual performance as it relates to staff agreements and meeting norms remind teams of the importance of such work (see Tool 4.4: Using Staff Agreements and Meeting Norms).

A teacher survey (Boston Consulting Group, 2014) reported that teachers that rank PLC time as one of their least preferred professional learning options. In considering the results, one possible reason for that finding is that in too many schools teachers had one view of PLCs and administrators had another. Similar complaints can be heard about faculty meetings and even school leadership team meetings. Using effective procedures and protocols signals to educators and other participants that their time is valued and will be used to accomplish important work.

Figure 4.1: The Learning Cycle Framework (see p. 61) offers a continuous improvement process including multiple protocols to guide the work that takes place within each stage. Learning design expertise is essential to the successful completion of Stages 3, 4, and 5. During Stage 3 Learning Individually and Collectively, grade-level or subject-matter teams engage in curriculum-based professional learning, investing the majority of their time in studying the instructional materials for upcoming units. During that time, they dig deeply into curriculum materials and they may take turns wearing a "student hat" as other team members rehearse upcoming lessons. They use these experiences to gain insights into how students may approach the lesson and they, as teachers, might modify lessons to help students learn.

The need for additional knowledge and skills is likely to surface during Stage 4 Implementation and Stage 5 Monitor and Adjust. Classroom observations may uncover when teachers face challenges with instructional practices in individual classrooms. Formative assessments that look at student work and unit tests may signal which students continue to struggle. Administering such ongoing, interim assessments can help teachers determine when different approaches may be needed to help students achieve on-grade level performance. When these new needs surface, the

DESIGNING LEARNING

Figure 4.1: The Learning Cycle Framework

Analyze data

Examine student and educator learning challenges:
- Identify and collect essential data
- Organize and display data for analysis
- Examine data for trends, issues, and opportunities
- Summarize the data

Monitor, assess, and adjust practice

Use evidence to assess and refine implementation and impact:
- Collect formative and summative data
- Monitor progress toward goals
- Analyze data and reflect on outcomes
- Refine and determine next actions

Set goals

Identify shared goals for student and educator learning:
- Review summary statements and set priorities
- Write student goals
- Write teacher goals
- Review with others

Implement new learning

Implement refined lessons and assessments with local support in the classroom:
- Develop plan for implementing units and lessons
- Use tools or resources to guide implementation and support adaptation as necessary
- Enlist job-embedded support
- Engage in feedback process with evidence from others to inform continuous improvement

Learn individually and collaboratively

Gain new knowledge and skills; examine assumptions, aspirations, and beliefs:
- Set learning priorities
- Write team and individual learning agendas
- Practice new learning
- Schedule and engage in learning

Source: Reprinted with permission, *Becoming a Learning Team: A Guide to a Teacher-led Cycle of Continuous Improvement*, Second edition, p. 18, by S. Hirsh and T. Crow. Copyright 2018 Learning Forward.

CHAPTER 4

Shared journey leads to engaged adult learning

In my six years at Croninger Elementary, the staff and I have taken a journey through professional learning designs from the traditional "sit-and-get" to collaborative assessment and learning in professional learning communities. We took our first step by using a simplified teaching and learning cycle with our adult learners, the teachers. The building coach and I collected observational data of the input and energy exerted by staff during and after a structured professional learning session. We found evidence of low participation, disengagement, and negative feedback, especially from primary-grade teachers. After analyzing the data, we determined that we needed to differentiate the learning for each group. So, first we created two cross-level teams, grades K–2 and 3–5. The split allowed us to address curriculum needs of each team by tailoring the professional learning to grade level.

We next made a goal to reform our current practice of providing weekly whole-group professional learning. We realized that if we wanted teachers to be more engaged, we needed to make learning time meaningful to teachers' daily practice so they would carry over the learning and implement it in their classrooms.

We focused our walk-through observations on the professional learning to see exactly how well teachers understood what they had learned and at what level they were able to incorporate new learnings into their practice. The teacher teams used — and we continue to use — the Concerns-based Adoption Model (CBAM) Stages of Concern and Levels of Use diagnostic tools to help them analyze their practice in their respective classrooms and in team collaborative learning sessions. The coach and I also used the CBAM tools to initiate our own thinking and questions about levels of support teachers might need. Targeted observations during team sessions and walk-throughs offered me opportunities to give specific and timely feedback and encourage the growth I could see.

Taking a closer look at each individual's and team's learning style was also a key step in building the cycle. The coach and I asked ourselves: Is our approach appropriate? Do the topics represent what we observed that teachers need? How could we better match teachers' needs so we might engage our adult learners to get results outside professional learning sessions? We used the KASAB protocol to focus as we guided team members toward understanding how the new learning fit into their daily practice. After each session, we reviewed and reflected on the format and presentation style to decide what would be appropriate for later use. More importantly, team members committed to apply their new learning in their classrooms. They chose a date when they would return to the group and share what they had learned as they implemented new practices, lessons, or instructional activities. This step was probably the hardest for teachers to take because it meant they opened up their classrooms and made themselves visible and vulnerable to their peers and me.

Finding out what your staff values for student learning — and their own — can be difficult. By routinely using learning designs such as classroom observations, team collaborative sessions, and individual-focused feedback meetings, we have refined a learning cycle that helps me gather data so I better understand my adult learners. I can build upon their values and encourage growth mindsets to lay the groundwork for sustained, continuous professional learning.

— *Carrie Kennedy*

Principal Carrie Kennedy (top, center) reviews a learning cycle with teacher learning team.

DESIGNING LEARNING

team or individuals circle back to Stage 3 to plan for additional learning. Some individuals may supplement their learning plans with more intensive coaching, model teaching, or co-teaching. Likewise, the entire team may need to invest in a technical assistance partner's guidance to be able to scaffold learning for particular groups of students. Teams that skimp on the learning stage will not achieve the goals set out in Stage 2 Set Goals and may waste valuable time and resources.

Team members consider many characteristics, conditions, and learning outcomes when they evaluate learning designs. During their research, teams find that some designs appear to be innovative and exciting, but they may not offer the depth or appropriate set of experiences essential to altering beliefs and practices. For example, conducting a book study on differentiation will make minor impact on teacher practice compared to observing another teacher with expertise in differentiation. Watching a video may expose new ideas but watching a video and debriefing the learning with a coach is more likely to produce clear actions. Knowing the strengths and weaknesses of various learning designs allows principals to guide teams toward making more efficient and effective choices.

4. Give voice and choice

More than a decade ago, the Gallup Poll unveiled the results of a landmark 30-year research project on the topic of leadership. They studied more than a million work teams, conducted in-depth interviews with more than 20,000 leaders around the world, and interviewed more than 10,000 of their followers to ask exactly *why* they followed the most important leader in their life. Tom Rath and Barry Conchie (2009) shared the results of their research: Know your strengths, get people with the right strengths on your team, and invest in building their strengths. Learning

principals know that bringing out the best of each staff member contributes to the overall success of the school. While preaching the shared vision, they recognize the importance of balancing that vision with individual voice and choice.

Vella's (1994) first learning principle, needs assessment, reinforces the importance of "listening to learners' wants and needs to shape professional learning that has immediate usefulness to adults." Needs assessments under the right circumstances can offer a strategy for giving voice to individuals. At the same time, they do not necessarily translate into an open invitation. Needs assessments aligned with school vision, goals, and priorities provide insights into the subject, issues, and processes that matter most to staff members. Learning principals' deep knowledge of various learning designs enables them to create learning experiences that are relevant and meaningful provide choice and honor voice of learners.

Learning principals also address voice and choice through the different opportunities for leadership and learning they create for educators at different career stages (Krupp,1987; Vella,1994). Entry-level teachers may voice concerns about needing more day-to-day support from a mentor or coach. They may want more time to observe exemplar teachers. They may seek more frequent feedback from principals and coaches. These requests that can be easily honored by principals and may also contribute to staff satisfaction and effectiveness. More experienced teachers may voice interests in expanding responsibilities and seeking leadership opportunities. They may seek support for attending professional conferences, gaining skills necessary to lead learning teams, or serving on school-level leadership committees. Honoring such requests may also contribute to staff satisfaction as well as retention. See Tool 4.5: Honoring Voice and Choice for a framework that helps with these decisions.

Ultimately, honoring voice and choice requires resources. Principals may consider allocating a percentage of funding for professional learning to school and team needs and another percentage for individual requests. To manage all requests, learning principals create procedures and criteria that are viewed by all as fair and equitable.

5. Understand high-quality professional learning

As leaders of continuous improvement in their schools, learning principals stay in touch with the latest information about professional learning that leads to the high goals they set with their teams for all students. In addition to knowing and implementing the Standards for Professional Learning, they ensure that their colleagues understand the "whys" behind the steps they take to leverage various learning designs appropriately.

Learning principals also familiarize themselves with recent research related to professional learning, particularly when it is related to the highest priorities identified for the school or to sharpen their use of learning designs. For example, when new studies about coaching emerge, they seek to understand if findings inform how they are using coaching in their context.

Learning principals may partner with district staff or coaches in their schools to stay abreast of the latest news as well as subscribe to relevant journals, email updates, and keeping their reading list current. Many learning principals are active in professional networks and organizations recognizing the value of learning from and with colleagues in similar as well as very different settings.

Conclusion

The Leadership standard (Learning Forward, 2011) calls on leaders

> to clearly articulate the critical link between increased student learning and educator professional learning. As supporters of professional learning, they apply understanding of organizational and human changes to design needed conditions, resources, and other supports for learning and change. (p. 29)

Effective school leaders focus on both the learning of individuals and the community of learners. As Andy Hargreaves and Michael Fullan (2012) point out in their book, *Professional Capital,* no single individual can learn enough on his own to ensure the success of every student. Instead, they suggest that "collaborative cultures build social capital and therefore also professional capital in a school community" (p. 114). They further describe collaborative cultures,

> They accumulate and circulate knowledge and ideas, as well as assistance and support, that help teachers become more effective, increase their confidence, and encourage them to be more open to and actively engaged in improvement and change. (p. 114)

In such a culture every team or community becomes a learning laboratory in which everyone comes to understand and support the learning goal(s) of the group.

To summarize, the most critical component of powerful designs is the connection of the learning of adults to the essential learning students need. For all students to learn what they need to learn well and at high levels, professional learning must be held to high standards. As communities of learners develop a strong sense of community, they initiate their journey of continuous improvement and build collective

DESIGNING LEARNING

Reflections

- What will I explore further about adult learners and learning designs? How will I do it?

- Would new or revised staff agreements or meeting norms be helpful to my learning agenda? If so, what actions might I take next?

- How will I establish and maintain a connection between equity and professional learning?

- How will I incorporate voice and choice into our schoolwide learning agendas?

- What would strengthen the learning agenda and learning team cycles at our school? How will I implement these shifts?

responsibility for student outcomes. Their moral purpose is strengthened as they work together and build on each other's strengths. Educators use data to understand where they are and establish challenging goals to inspire them to continue to learn from each other, from the larger community of educators, and from their students. As they make progress and celebrate their successes, they develop confidence in themselves, take greater risks, and are never content with the status quo. Learning principals set the stage for such learning and participate daily as both leaders and learners themselves.

References

Boston Consulting Group. (2014). *Teachers know best: Teachers' views on professional development.* Bill & Melinda Gates Foundation. Available at https://k12education.gatesfoundation.org/download/?Num=2336&filename=Gates-PDMarketResearch-Dec5.pdf

Easton, L. B. (Ed.). (2015). *Powerful designs for professional learning* (3rd ed.). Learning Forward.

Gregorc, A. (1984). *Gregorc style delineator:*

Development, technical, and administration manual. Gregorc Associates.

Hargreaves, A. & Fullan, M. (2012). *Professional capital: Transforming teaching in every school.* Teachers College Press.

Hirsh, S. & Crow, T. (2017). *Becoming a learning team: A guide to a teacher-led cycle of continuous improvement* (2nd ed.). Learning Forward.

Hirsh, S., Psencik, K., & Brown, F. (2018). *Becoming a learning system* (Revised ed.). Learning Forward.

Joyce, B. & Showers, B. (2002). *Student achievement through staff development* (3rd ed.). Association for Supervision and Curriculum Development.

Joyce, B., Weil, M., & Calhoun, E. (2015). *Models of teaching* (9th ed.). Pearson.

Kendi, I.X. (2019). *How to be an antiracist.* One World.

Knowles, M.S. (1984). *Andragogy in action.* Jossey Bass.

Krupp, J.A. (1987). Understanding and motivating personnel in the second half of life. *Journal of Education, 169*(1), 20–46.

CHAPTER 4

Learning Forward. (2011). *Standards for Professional Learning.* Author.

Rath, T. & Conchie, B. (2009). *Strengths-based leadership.* Gallup Press.

Singleton, G. (2015). *Courageous conversations about race: A field guide for achieving equity in schools.* (2nd ed.) Corwin.

Sparks, D. & Loucks-Horsley, S. (1989). *Five models of staff development for teachers.* Journal of Staff Development,10(4), 40–57.

Vella, J. (1994). *Learning to listen, learning to teach: The power of dialogue in educating adults.* Jossey Bass.

The Wallace Foundation. (2013). *The school principal as leader: Guiding schools to better teaching and learning.* Author.

Tools index for Chapter 4

Tool	Title	Use
4.1	Selecting a Learning Design	This tool helps principals and teacher teams evaluate various learning designs for their strength in addressing challenges identified during the learning cycle.
4.2	Designing a Learning Agenda	This tool guides the development of a comprehensive learning agenda for the school.
4.3	Advancing Equity	This tool lets principals examine the content and contexts of professional learning for beliefs, practices, and systems that support or hinder all students' opportunities to learn.
4.4	Using Staff Agreements and Meeting Norms	This tool supports the development or refinement of staff and meeting norms.
4.5	Honoring Voice and Choice	This tool helps develop growth plans that represent individual needs and choices.

CHAPTER 5

Maximizing resources

Where are we now?

The principal recognizes the important contribution of each resource to the school vision and mission.

STRONGLY AGREE	AGREE	NO OPINION	DISAGREE	STRONGLY DISAGREE

The principal leverages key resources including human capital (staff), technology, high-quality instructional materials, and time to advance equity and excellence.

STRONGLY AGREE	AGREE	NO OPINION	DISAGREE	STRONGLY DISAGREE

The principal organizes time to ensure all educators are deeply engaged in learning teams and observation cycles with peers.

STRONGLY AGREE	AGREE	NO OPINION	DISAGREE	STRONGLY DISAGREE

The principal uses technology and facilitates its use to personalize and accommodate student and educator interests and needs.

STRONGLY AGREE	AGREE	NO OPINION	DISAGREE	STRONGLY DISAGREE

The principal shares leadership with staff members to maximize the human capital resources within the school.

STRONGLY AGREE	AGREE	NO OPINION	DISAGREE	STRONGLY DISAGREE

CHAPTER 5

Every principal needs to consider herself a learning principal to ensure the success of the staff and students in the school. One of the tenets that I adhere to is this: "If you ever believe that you have nothing more to learn, you may need to consider a different career path." There is always something to learn that will prepare you and those around you to better serve your students. As learning leaders, we must model for our staff and students what it means to have a constant thirst for new learning and what they need to do to quench that thirst.

Stephanie Montez
Principal, Adams Elementary
Mesa Public Schools
Mesa, Arizona

Overview

The availability and distribution of resources to schools stand as two of the most critical equity issues for educators and students today. Policymakers at federal and provincial or state levels have the responsibility to ensure that education funding systems both give school communities equitable access to resources for learning and distribute those funds where they are needed. Yet, it is the learning principals who have the responsibility to ensure that they distribute their existing resources in ways that maximize support for educators and accelerate outcomes for students.

This chapter focuses on how learning principals leverage school resources to produce high levels of learning and performance in their schools. Every system provides principals with resources to support school operations. Resources range from actual funds in the school-level budget, to staffing positions, instructional materials, technology allotments, and more. Learning principals study carefully all resources available to them so that they know what they will be able to work with to carry out the school mission. Savvy principals also look for available resources beyond those provided by the school system.

Specifically, learning principals ensure that resources are allocated to advance learning as the core work of their schools. They accomplish this allocation process by establishing several expectations and structures in their schools. First, as previously discussed, learning schools are organized so that all students are the shared responsibility of every teacher and staff member who interacts with those students, including classroom teachers, special area teachers, specialists, and counselors. Second, all educators belong to learning teams that share collective responsibility for the success of all students assigned to the team.

The teacher learning team and school leadership teams are structures through which learning principals share decision making with teacher leaders and others about how resources are best allocated. Learning principals prioritize resources to ensure educators have the time, instructional materials, and support they need for high-functioning learning teams that produce great outcomes for students.

Resources are essential

The Learning Forward (2011) Standards for Professional Learning point out the importance of resources to achieving desired outcomes for adults and students.

> Effective professional learning requires human, fiscal, material, technology, and time resources to achieve student learning goals. How resources are allocated for professional learning can overcome inequities and achieve results for educators and students. The availability and allocation of resources for professional learning affect its quality and results. Understanding the resources associated with professional learning and actively and accurately tracking them facilitates better decisions about and increased quality and results of professional learning. (p. 32)

Resources to support professional learning include personnel, materials, technology, and time. Decisions about resources for professional learning require a thoughtful consideration of student and educator learning needs, clear commitment to ensure equity in resource allocation, and thorough understanding of various strategies selected to achieve the intended outcomes for students and educators.

The key resources

Personnel is the largest expense item in any school budget. In learning schools, principals use discretion in hiring and assigning staff to advance learning priorities and improve practice. They determine which staffing arrangements will best serve the needs of their faculty and students. For example, a principal whose staff includes a significant number of new teachers may choose to use additional staffing dollars to provide intensive mentoring for new staff members. Or, a school that is implementing a new science curriculum may require specialized coaching to support the important changes that need to take place in classrooms. Another way a principal leverages staffing resources might be recognizing that learning teams need a balance among years of experience, gender, racial and cultural diversity, and expertise of its members. As a result, the principal realizes that some teachers may require additional support as they make transitions to new grade levels or courses. Hiring and assigning substitutes to cover classrooms when teachers benefit from more extended learning opportunities can also be considered a personnel cost. These are just a few of the examples that represent the kinds of decisions principals may make in relation to their allocation of personnel resources.

Principals also allocate time, another extremely valuable resource, particularly for professional learning. Education systems worldwide ensure teachers have substantive time during the school day for teacher planning, collaboration, and classroom-based support to increase student learning. Their learning agendas align with school, team, and individual goals. Core learning happens daily among teams of teachers who share collective responsibility for the success of the students served by the team. Educators engage in other learning in classrooms through modeling and co-teaching as well as observation and feedback cycles. Learning time for educators may extend into after-school meetings, summer extended learning experiences, and occasional times during the workday when students are not present. Learning principals are skilled in balancing various uses of time and arranging schedules that make appropriate learning designs available to all educators.

Technology and other instructional resources are foundational in advancing equity and excellence in schools. In particular, high-quality instructional materials ensure that teachers have essential guidance and students have powerful tools for addressing the system's academic standards and guidance for differentiating instruction for students who need extra help or those who need acceleration opportunities. In the absence of available standards-based resources, teachers need learning experiences that enable them to identify and select appropriate standards-aligned materials for use in the classroom.

One lesson from the 2020 COVID-19 pandemic was that equipping schools, teachers, and students with technology to connect with one another and with digital resources is nonnegotiable. Even when schools are functioning largely face to face, classroom technology that supports teachers and students increases planning efficiencies when teachers can plan, implement, and monitor instruction and assessments to meet individual needs and interests. As technology becomes the primary means of learning for adults and students alike, schools and systems are responsible for universal access. Leaders may raise the priority of expenditures that are intended to ensure everyone involved can use the technology for its intended purposes.

Innovative technologies provide powerful new professional learning opportunities. Earbud technologies enable teachers to access just-in-time coaching; classroom video captures and transfer make it incredibly easy for teachers to connect with colleagues, mentors, and coaches and discuss teaching in the classroom. Colleagues can use this information to monitor and assess progress toward educator and student learning outcomes.

Finally, other resources, such as funds to engage external support, have an impact on professional learning. External support may include content experts to help teachers develop deeper understanding and technical skills for implementing changes. Or, it may cover skilled individuals who provide classroom-based coaching and job-embedded professional learning. External support in both of these forms may be located in local universities, professional associations, and sometimes district and school retirees.

Other related resources include fees for course tuition, program registrations, and conference expenses. Given the importance of sustaining learning over time, there is skepticism on the value of these expenditures. While long-term change requires much more than short courses, workshops, and conferences, they can play a role in supporting individual needs, inspiring new ideas, and helping educators stay on the cutting edge of what works best in meeting student needs.

Leveraging and monitoring resources

Although the main source of resources for professional learning is likely the school district, the sources of origin include federal, state, and local funding organizations. Some principals are able to tap additional funding sources including philanthropic organizations. Learning principals are also keenly aware of the resources that can be accessed through local universities, regional education agencies, and state and federal comprehensive assistance centers. Amassing and organizing resources can be demanding;

MAXIMIZING RESOURCES

even the most entrepreneurial principal will never have all the resources necessary to meet their needs.

As a result, a learning principal develops strategies for prioritizing and allocating resources to maximize outcomes. The path to maximizing resources is simpler when the principal has a few basic school improvement strategies in place in the school. First and foremost are a school vision, mission, and a limited number of improvement priorities. While there will never be a shortage of issues that demand attention, no school, no matter how small or large, can truly focus on more than two to three big initiatives each school year. Major changes like shifting to new content standards or assessment systems will take more than one year to effectively institutionalize. In the most aligned and coherent schools, strong statements of school priorities provide clear direction and opportunities for focus for team and individual learning.

Principals benefit from creating practical systems for monitoring use and impact of their resource investments. Tracking and monitoring resources is important when learning principals are committed to ensuring resources are being used as planned and for understanding why changes are made. Such systems provide valuable data to school and team leaders for assessing and adjusting their ongoing plans for improvement. At times, principals may receive inquiries regarding resource allocation decisions, and they would be well served to have accessible data on the impact of those decisions. Parents questioning the use of early-release days for professional learning, for example, might benefit from information that explains to them how teachers are spending time and how students benefit from changes made in the classroom as a result. With their every resource under careful scrutiny, principals have a responsibility to apply monitoring and reporting systems carefully and widely share results.

Taking action

While many decisions related to the acquisition and allocation of resources may seem out of the reach of the principal, principals have many opportunities to influence their acquisition and use. Managing those key decisions will accelerate a school's progress. Learning principals can use the five strategies below to strengthen their use of resources.

1. Coordinate and prioritize resources

Being fully aware of the resources that exist within the school is key to a principal's effective deployment and management of them. While resources fall into many categories (e.g. operations, student support), a learning principal pays particular attention to the resources that can be leveraged to build capacity of the educators and others who play a role in advancing student learning. Taking an inventory of such resources allows a principal to see the full range of opportunities to access. Engaging others in the process increases staff awareness and potential desire and commitment to see resources allocated so that they lead to better outcomes.

Conducting such an inventory involves defining the resources to be inventoried. The following categories are one place to begin:

- Personnel units;
- Stipends for additional assignments (e.g. department chair);
- Time allocated for professional learning;
- Time allocated for individual planning;
- Time allocated for faculty meetings;
- Dollars available for instructional materials and technology;
- Dollars allocated for external "trainers" or experts;

www.learningforward.org

The LEARNING PRINCIPAL **71**

CHAPTER 5

- Dollars allocated for compensating internal experts who assume new responsibilities;
- Funding for conference attendance, course, and workshop fees;
- Other funding sources for district and state programming.

See Tool 5.1: Inventorying Learning Resources and Maximizing Their Use to guide data collection and analysis.

Once the learning principal and staff share a clear understanding about where flexibility and opportunity exist within their available resources, their discussion shifts to determining the priorities that require the most resources. The issue of determining school goals and priorities has been addressed in previous chapters and this process can identify how to deploy resources toward higher priorities. Concurrently, this important discussion likely also leads to the abandonment of initiatives of lesser importance and thus resources will no longer be attached to them.

Learning principals are constantly seeking and identifying opportunities to build capacity of those responsible for the success of the school. Engaging a diverse group of stakeholders in this process establishes new expertise and potential advocates for any changes leaders deem necessary and valuable. Recent research has documented the impact of shared decision making on student achievement, and allocating resources is one of the most important areas that demands understanding, attention, and commitment from an entire community.

Richard Ingersoll, Patrick Dougherty, and Phil Sirinides (2017) drew on findings from the NTC's Teaching, Empowering, Leading and Learning (TELL) Survey. Their analysis was the first national, representative single dataset from the TELL Survey to examine which educator and school variables correlate with student achievement. In analyzing responses

from the TELL Survey from 2011 to 2015, they examined data from more than one million teachers and principals in more than 25,000 schools, representing 16 states. Two findings are that 1) students perform better in schools with the highest levels of instructional and teacher leadership; and 2) the degree to which teachers were involved in school governance affected student learning substantially. In both mathematics and English Language Arts (ELA), the school with the highest teacher participation in governance was ranked at the 56th percentile. Conversely, a school with the least teacher participation was ranked at the 45th percentile in both mathematics and ELA proficiency.

2. Leverage expertise of the best teachers

"School systems typically provide few formal opportunities for teacher leadership roles, and they invest little to develop teacher leadership" (Hawley-Miles, Sommers, Roy, & von Frank, 2016, p. 26). But research has shown that providing opportunities for the most effective teachers to extend their reach can encourage a teacher's professional growth, incentivize and reward performance, and increase retention of the most effective teachers without requiring broad changes to compensation models (Hanushek & Rivkin, 2007).

Hirsh and Killion (2009) wrote: "Communities can solve their most complex problems by tapping internal expertise" (p. 468). For too many years principals have been asked to look outside the school to address their priorities and challenges. Rarely are they asked whether they have tapped the expertise of those teachers experiencing success within their schools.

Hirsh and Killion (2009) go on to say:

Answers, we contend, lie within the community

Creating a learning culture
Pineapple means "Welcome" to learn in classrooms

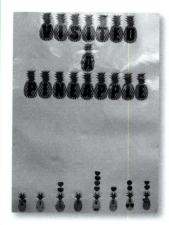

At Adams Elementary school, we believe that every person needs to model a growth mindset by being a consummate learner. We administrators prioritize time to ensure that teachers can observe and learn from one another. As a result, our teachers are learning constantly from one another and showing the students that they are learning. One way in which the leadership team supports teacher learning is to help create **subject matter experts**. That idea works this way: In addition to their schoolwide ELA and math goals, each grade-level team chooses one SMART goal about which they will become experts by the end of the year. Teachers first analyze their data and identify one item that the entire grade level will learn. It might be sight words, addition strategies, or integrating literacy and math. Then, after picking their topic, they develop a resource list. The leadership team helps them get what they'll need to become experts.

While the grade-level teams are learning about their growth area, they open their classrooms to anyone to observe and share feedback. We adapted a practice called "pineappling" your classroom. We created a chart in the teachers' lounge where a teacher can write which strategy they are using and when they'll be trying it so other teachers know they can visit. Administrators cover the classes of anyone who wants to visit. As an additional incentive, we give prizes to the teachers who pineapple their rooms or go visit a pineapple. Students understand that when another teacher is visiting a room that they are engaged in learning from each another. Being able to see learning happen and to be part of it has really helped students — and our entire building — value learning. Our teachers appreciate one another even

Principal Stephanie Montez welcomes students to another day of learning.

more! There are many times when I have shown my own vulnerability; I express that I am still learning and have found ways to improve. When everyone in the building is learning new things, we all benefit — especially the students!

— *Stephanie Montez*

CHAPTER 5

in which the problems exist. Educators have a penchant for depending on external expertise to solve their challenging problems. This form of dependency has taken its toll on both individuals and systems. Individuals in dependency-prone environments lose their identity as professionals and become complicit workers, which removes individual commitment and investment. For systems, dependency leads to a revolving door of innovations, most with substantial costs and recycled practices that have been renamed to fit the particular reform they accompany. (p. 468)

Effective leaders know how to identify, cultivate, and tap the internal expertise of members of their staff in order to unleash potential and use expertise in new and powerful ways. Giving effective teachers leadership roles extends their reach to more students and teachers and likely will have a significant effect on student performance According to Public Impact (2014–2019), "Schools that consistently provide all students with excellent teachers — those in today's top 20 to 25 percent who achieve well over *one year of learning progress*" — can close most achievement gaps over two to four years (p. 4).

But, the report adds, "most schools provide students with teaching at this level in only one of four classrooms" (p. 4). Learning principals can extend the reach of effective teachers by tapping them to lead multiclassroom teaching teams, model collaborative use of technologies, mentor new teachers, and so on. In shifting from the use of external experts to volunteers and internal experts (see Table 5.1, p. 75), principals find that intentional recruiting and assignment can "provide teachers with career opportunities that also improve student learning" (Public Impact, 2014–2019, p. 4). See Tool 5.2: Leveraging Internal Expertise to dig more deeply into these examples and others.

Collective impact occurs when each individual feels a responsibility for sharing expertise and leadership with others. When collective impact is at its best in schools, teachers take advantage of the leadership and expertise of their colleagues and all students benefit.

3. Conduct a time study

Over the years and through countless polls and surveys, *time* is the one resource mentioned consistently by principals and others as a limitation to school staff members' achieving all their learning goals. In fact, finding time for job-embedded professional learning is one of the most frequently cited challenges with implementing change in education (ASCD, 2012; MetLife, 2012, 2013; Scholastic Press & Bill & Melinda Gates Foundation, 2011). Principals and teachers alike lament the lack of time to address everything on their overflowing plates of priorities. In other nations that outperform the U.S., students have less instructional time and teachers have substantially more time for collaborative professional learning (Wei, Darling-Hammond, Richardson, Andree, & Orphanos, 2009). The principal, however, has the power to influence the calendar:

The first thing to understand is that schedules are not sacred. . . . . As a former principal, I understand that factors such as our stomachs and yellow buses sometimes dictate the schedule. All too often, however, schedules are geared to what is best for the bus drivers and cafeteria workers' schedules… rather than being geared to what is best for students and teachers. My point is that a schedule is not what enables or disables collaborative professional learning. It is the top-down commitment to professional

74 The LEARNING PRINCIPAL

Learning Forward

MAXIMIZING RESOURCES

Table 5.1: Practices that Extend the Reach of Effective Teachers

Moving from	To	Results in
Elected school leadership team composition	Combination of elected and appointed	• Retention of the types of representatives needed to ensure buy-in for a given change. • Opportunity to bring in voices that offer identified expertise. • Opportunity to give selected teachers leadership opportunities.
External consultants to lead professional learning	Teachers with demonstrated expertise in identified areas of need leading professional learning	• Credibility established quickly. • Diverting resources to internal staff, a move that can also help retain experts within the school.
Hiring external coaches to provide classroom-based support	Identification of coaches from existing staff members who have demonstrated success with the priorities	• Credibility established quickly. • Resources diverted to compensate internal staff members, a move that can also help retain experts within the school. • Continual assessment and reprioritizing of coaching needs gives different individuals opportunities to serve as coach. • Coaches who return to classrooms have grown as teachers.
Grade-level and subject/department leads assigned by seniority	Grade-level and subject/department leads recruited with intentionality	• Creation of leadership opportunities and career ladders that contribute to retention. • Professional learning for these leaders builds internal capacity. • Contribution to pipeline for other in-school leadership opportunities.
Mentor assignments for student teachers, residents, and first-year teachers made based on teacher volunteers	Mentors identified based on careful screening criteria, including interviews by teachers	• Creation of leadership opportunities that contribute to retention. • Opportunities such as mentoring, coaching, team leads, leadership team service can potentially be components of a career ladder. • Mentor professional learning builds internal capacity. • Contribution to pipeline for other in-school leadership opportunities.

CHAPTER 5

learning, or lack thereof, that promotes or hinders collaborative professional learning. … Collaborative professional learning does not begin with plans for a schedule change but with commitment to a cultural change.

— *Jack Linton, assistant superintendent,*
Petal School District, Petal, Mississippi
(Killion, 2013, p. 4)

Learning principals can use the authority they have to allocate staff and time to best accomplish school learning priorities. Many begin by looking to repurpose existing time. Yet, it is hard to repurpose what is not fully understood. So an important step is collecting data on all the ways time is allocated and used by professionals in the school. Learning principals who engage with staff members in a deliberate process of data gathering and analysis can produce the shared foundational information necessary to recommending changes for the future. See Tool 5.3: Finding Time for Professional Learning for one approach to this process.

Learning principals also engage external stakeholders in the development of and advocacy for new schedules. For many reasons, families and community members are invested in the existing school schedule. They use it to plan, sometimes years in advance, for vacations and child care. Some believe that sacrificing student learning time for educator learning time will have a negative impact on academic progress. At the same time, teacher complaints over the years about professional learning does not motivate them to support a greater investment in it. Changing stakeholders' attitudes and beliefs requires advocacy by key representatives who have widespread credibility and are well prepared to speak to the issues and questions they will face. These representatives must have a deep understanding of the purpose for professional learning and benefits to students from teacher learning

and know how to talk about it skillfully with a range of audiences.

Through the process, stakeholders may come to understand that not all allocated student time is actually academic learning time, and that a careful repurposing of that time to increase professional learning and collaboration can accelerate achievement of learning goals. Opportunities to study how other schools allocate time and the results of their efforts will help them see new options for their school. Stakeholders may choose to champion new possibilities for allocating time and adjusting the current schedule.

Time is one of the greatest resource challenges to principals. Collaboratively developing a plan for increasing time toward commonly embraced priorities can establish the foundation for maintaining a commitment to ongoing learning and improvement in schools.

4. Provide access to high-quality instructional materials and technology

As covered throughout this book, studying and implementing high-quality instructional materials as the anchor for the work of effective learning teams is an essential pathway to school improvement. Learning principals remind school system leaders of their responsibility to provide such resources to their teachers. Choosing high-quality instructional materials is not a decision to be made school by school. It is a decision that affects equity and excellence for every student. Principals can advocate for school representation on selection committees, which ultimately contributes to greater expertise on their campus. Having highly respected and effective teachers engaged in the process builds trust and acceptance for the changes that will result after decisions about materials are made.

In the absence of high-quality instructional materials, principals ensure that teachers have sufficient understanding of academic standards to be able to locate and judge appropriate resources. In these situations, learning principals provide professional learning to help teachers locate and evaluate available materials for alignment and appropriateness for the classroom. Ongoing investments in such learning will be necessary when standards are revised or new members join the team.

As educators embrace the research endorsing the positive impact that high-quality materials and related professional learning have on learning, their investments will pay off. As more of these materials become available for free or at low cost, a growing number of principals will be able to invest in the professional learning needed to ensure effective implementation and meet other school priorities.

Learning principals also ensure access to high-speed broadband, web-based technologies, professional journals, books, software applications, and other subscriptions. They and their decision-making teams select technologies that use interactive learning processes to engage learners in acquiring knowledge and skills, refining practice, and developing dispositions. Giving individuals and teams of educators access to learning resources and participation in local or global communities or networks promotes continuous learning and improvement (Killion & Hirsh, 2012).

5. Monitor and report on the impact of new investments

Finally, principals know that questions will surface when resources are shifted to new priorities. Skeptics may dismiss any new effort as merely the flavor of the month. Some staff members or stakeholders will wonder whether the shifts will make any difference.

Those attached to existing programs and services will want evidence that the decision to shift funding to new initiatives would benefit educators and students more than the currently funded efforts. In response, change-focused principals will communicate early wins with those who supported the shifts and those who questioned them.

Early wins are equally important for building credibility and potential flexibility in those areas where reallocation of resources is more restrictive. Principals and leadership teams may use the resources and tools attached to the logic model for documenting impacts of professional learning as the foundation for collecting these data (see Chapter 3: Managing Change). They act deliberately to report changes in resource allocation. They use examples drawn from data about teaching practice and student outcomes to demonstrate the program or strategy supported by the change, identify the persons and students served, and show evidence of how they benefit. Amplifying the process and results will contribute to the rationale and potentially build the demand for continuing the process for leveraging all resources to achieve the school vision and mission.

Conclusion

Learning principals leverage school resources to produce high levels of learning and performance in their schools. They establish expectations and structures through which they allocate resources ranging from staff positions and instructional materials to technology allotments, time, and more. They inventory, prioritize, and leverage resources so they can extend the expertise of teachers and provide access to high-quality instructional materials. They look beyond the district for resources. Finally, learning principals monitor and report on the impact of new investments.

CHAPTER 5

Reflections

- What resources can I leverage to realize the school vision and achieve its mission?

- How can I engage staff and community stakeholders to impact the allocation of resources?

- Do I see new possibilities for arranging time to support capacity building of educators and other key stakeholders?

- What is the role that high-quality instructional materials play in supporting effective teaching in my school?

- What new possibilities might I consider for aligning resources to school priorities? What are potential costs and benefits?

References

ASCD. (2012). *Fulfilling the promise of Common Core State Standards: Moving from adoption to implementation.* Author.

Hanushek, E. & Rivkin, S. (2007). Pay, working conditions, teacher quality. *The Future of Children, 7*(1), 69–86.

Hawley-Miles, K., Sommers, A., Roy, P., & von Frank, V. (2016). *Reach the highest standard in professional learning: Resources.* Corwin.

Hirsh, S. & Killion, J. (2009, March). When educators learn, students learn: Eight principles of professional learning. *Phi Delta Kappan, 90*(7), 464–469.

Ingersoll, R. M., Dougherty, P., & Sirinides, P. (2017). *School leadership counts: Instructional leadership for student success.* New Teacher Center.

Killion, J. (2013). *Establishing time for professional learning.* Learning Forward.

Killion, J. & Hirsh, S. (2012). Analyze and plan professional learning investments. *JSD, 33*(1), 17–21

Learning Forward. (2011). *Standards for Professional Learning.* Author.

MetLife Inc. (2012). *The MetLife survey of the American teacher: Teachers, parents, and the economy.* Author. ED530021. Available at https://eric.ed.gov/?q=MetLife+teacher+survey+2006&id=ED530021

MetLife Inc. (2013). *The MetLife survey of the American teacher: Challenges in school leadership.* Author. ED542202. Available at https://eric.ed.gov/?q=MetLife+teacher+survey+2006&id=ED542202

Public Impact. (2014–2019). *Seizing opportunity at the top II: State policies to reach every student with excellent teaching.* Author. Available at http://opportunityculture.org/wp-content/uploads/2014/10/Seizing_Opportunity_at_the_Top_IIPublic_Impact.pdf

Scholastic & Bill & Melinda Gates Foundation. (2012). *Primary sources: 2012: America's teachers on the teaching profession.* Scholastic Press.

Wei, R.C., Darling-Hammond, L., Andree, A., Richardson, N., & Orphanos, S. (2009). *Professional learning in the learning profession: A status report on teacher development in the United States and abroad. Technical report.* National Staff Development Council.

Tools index for Chapter 5

Tool	Title	Use
5.1	Inventorying Learning Resources and Maximizing Their Use	This tool can be used to develop shared awareness and ownership for resources available to advance the school's learning agendas.
5.2	Leveraging Internal Expertise	This tool provides resources to help principals and school leaders leverage internal expertise to accelerate learning agendas.
5.3	Finding Time for Professional Learning	This tool helps principals examine how time is currently used across the school and determine strategies for adding or restructuring time for professional learning.

CHAPTER 6

Leveraging feedback and coaching

Where are we now?

The principal understands the role coaching plays in school, team, and individual improvement.

| STRONGLY AGREE | AGREE | NO OPINION | DISAGREE | STRONGLY DISAGREE |

The principal uses a variety of coaching strategies to support teacher and team growth.

| STRONGLY AGREE | AGREE | NO OPINION | DISAGREE | STRONGLY DISAGREE |

The principal monitors the impact of coaching and feedback conversations on shifts in educator practice.

| STRONGLY AGREE | AGREE | NO OPINION | DISAGREE | STRONGLY DISAGREE |

The principal ensures that all educators have access to appropriate and helpful feedback.

| STRONGLY AGREE | AGREE | NO OPINION | DISAGREE | STRONGLY DISAGREE |

The principal can articulate the distinction between the role of coach and appraiser; he knows how to shift, as needed, from one role to the other to address teacher learning needs.

| STRONGLY AGREE | AGREE | NO OPINION | DISAGREE | STRONGLY DISAGREE |

www.learningforward.org   The LEARNING PRINCIPAL   **81**

> *A learning principal is someone who engages in teaching and learning every single day and expects everyone in their building to be a learner as well. Whether facilitating professional learning communities on their campuses or engaging in meaningful, job-embedded professional learning, learning principals put* **learning** *at the forefront of everything that happens in their buildings. A learning principal can be found in classrooms engaging with students daily, asking questions that provoke deep thinking and reflection, and modeling what it means to be a lifelong learner. Learning principals continually look for new ways to foster the best possible learning environment for their teachers and students. In that way, I believe, learning principals inspire those in their buildings to improve and refine their craft.*
>
> Leslie Ceballos
> Assistant Principal, Dr. E.T. Boon Elementary
> Allen ISD
> Allen, Texas

Overview

Coaching is a powerful strategy that effective principals use to strengthen the learning and improvement process in schools. In the coaching role, principals create opportunities for deep conversations and rich learning experiences for both individual teachers and teacher teams. Effective coaching provides opportunities for feedback and reflection essential to thinking and learning.

The Learning Forward (2011) Standards for Professional Learning state that constructive feedback accelerates implementation of desired changes. It involves providing specific information "to assess practice in relationship to established expectations" (p. 46) and support for adjusting practice so that it more closely aligns with those expectations. Reflection is a form of feedback "in which a learner engages in providing constructive feedback on his or her own or others' practices" (p. 46). Principals promote reflection with teachers and teams of teachers and engage in reflection to advance their own learning.

Robert Hargrove (2008) author of *Masterful Coaching* describes a coach as someone who is *other-centered*; that coach values the person he is coaching as capable of making their own choices. Rather than direct, coaches inspire their coachees to achieve what they believe to be impossible. To do that, they focus their coaching on high-quality attention and listening. Such authentic listening gives the coach awareness of all the coachee's perspectives — the gifts they bring, the challenges they face, and the barriers they need to overcome to achieve their goals. A coach assists their coachees in seeing new possibilities and connecting new thinking and actions with their intentions.

The International Coaching Federation (ICF) defines coaching as "partnering with clients in a

LEVERAGING FEEDBACK AND COACHING

thought-provoking and creative process that inspires one to maximize their personal and professional potential" (para. 9). The process of coaching often unlocks previously untapped sources of imagination, productivity, and leadership. When a principal acts as coach, she may develop an understanding of her current state that may lead to openness and willingness to grow and learn.

To successfully fulfill their many responsibilities, learning principals play many roles. Acting as both appraiser and coach, they have the potential to affect the quality of teaching and learning in classrooms each day. Skillful learning principals, understandably, are sensitive to the intersection of those two roles. While they fulfill their appraisal responsibilities, they shift to coaching skills to support a growth mindset toward the improvements they want to promote. Likewise, learning principals use coaching to support teams as they implement their cycles of improvement.

Principals balance roles of appraiser and coach

All principals are accountable for executing their role as appraiser according to school system expectations, processes, and criteria. Learning principals apply their knowledge of adult learning and development as well as coaching to add value to the process. They see fulfillment of the appraisal requirements as only one aspect of a larger growth and development process they want for all teachers. A learning principal might begin the annual appraisal cycle by examining data with the teacher along with eliciting the educator's goals and desires. Together, they set student learning goals and the teacher's own goals. They align educator learning goals with the outcomes they seek for students. They define what an instructor needs to know and be able

to do to ensure that all students master standards. When principals consult with teachers to take into account teachers' strengths and interests while building a learning plan, they increase trust, commitment, and action. They may review where the teacher will get support in achieving goals through schoolwide and team learning experiences as well as potential opportunities for independent learning. As the principal offers to support educators' professional learning plans, they develop a partnership with their teachers. And when teachers recognize that the principal is invested in their success, they are more likely to trust and accept her support as a coach. Throughout the process, learning principals are committed to honing the skills vital to their success in the coaching role.

The principal and teachers continuously assess teacher and student performance and growth; they use that information to shape future learning priorities. Throughout the cycle, teachers benefit from feedback from supervisors, coaches, and colleagues. In the coaching role, principals provide feedback and facilitate reflection on the progress individuals are making toward their learning goals. They may use classroom videos and student surveys to anchor such conversations. Analysis and discussion of summative unit data provide another important opportunity for principals as coaches to monitor progress, celebrate success, or revisit the learning agenda if the desired progress is not evident. Monitoring progress toward goals and their impact on practice are important to success (Luczak, Perkins, Frades, & Morgan, 2015).

Learning principals view the individual appraisal process as a core component of the school improvement and learning agenda. They leverage the process to encourage ongoing educator growth and professional learning rather than to strictly measure

www.learningforward.org

The LEARNING PRINCIPAL **83**

past and predict future performance. Appraising with and through their coaching lens, principals sharpen their understanding and appreciation of staff strengths and where they need to focus individual, team, and schoolwide attention.

Learning principals coach teams and individuals

In learning schools all educators are committed to continuous improvement and collective responsibility for the success of every student. Learning principals support this commitment by ensuring there is schoolwide understanding, acceptance, and implementation of an ongoing improvement process. Yet, even with a shared commitment to the process, principals are well aware that challenges and barriers inhibit progress of teacher teams throughout the improvement cycle. Learning principals use various *coaching stances* to increase their productivity and help them overcome barriers.

Coaching stances generally refers to the approaches coaches take to working with individuals and teams. Several frameworks help coaches consider different stances for different situations. Joellen Killion (2007) describes three stances a coach may take in interactions with teachers: expert, peer, and facilitator. Laura Lipton and Bruce Wellman (2001; 2007) offer a process orientation in which the coach is consulting, collaborating, or mediating thinking. Kay Psencik's (2011) framework of coaching stances offers four approaches — mentoring, facilitative, collaborative/consultative, and mastery. Chris Bryan and Brenda Kaylor (2018) modified Lipton and Wellman's framework to consultant, collaborator, and coach of reflective thinking. All of these variations in stances describe coach-teacher or coach-team interactions ranging from direct instruction or demonstration to facilitative problem solving to reflective learning. A consultant, for example, may serve as an expert who provides solutions, teaches new techniques, or advises. A collaborator works as a partner to develop ideas, products, or solutions. Coaches mediate thinking when they facilitate metacognition and promote the learner's own reflection and problem solving.

Tool 6.1: Developing Coaching Skills and Understanding Stances draws on that literature to guide principals in deepening their understanding of coaching skills and applying different coaching stances. When principals act in the coaching role, they learn how to shift stances as needed to meet a teacher's learning need. Joellen Killion and Cindy Harrison (2017) indicate that deciding which stance to take in each situation is one of the most complex choices a coach faces. By virtue of their role, coach principals are most often viewed as consultants, yet learning principals prefer to work as collaborators and push toward being mediators. According to Killion and Harrison (2017),

> the ultimate goal of coaching is to increase student success by developing the capacity of educators to plan, reflect on, and analyze their practice so they can achieve consistently the desired results, use everyday situations as opportunities to learn and refine practice, and strengthen results over time. (p. 130)

Principals join team learning sessions to observe the progress they are making toward their goals as well as their adherence to the school's learning cycle. Sometimes principals may find no reason to engage. Simply listening and learning provides the information they seek. At other times, they may find a team is struggling and that they need to decide which stance to use to support the team in addressing a challenge so they may continue their work together.

Supporting and making the most of your instructional coach

Two years ago, I became assistant principal on an elementary campus that had the support of two campus instructional coaches for the first time. I was excited to join their journey because I had been a coach for the last five years and knew coaching can make a positive impact on teacher practice and student learning. The campus is a "veteran-heavy" campus where the majority of teachers have been in the profession and at the campus for 14+ years. Coaches were going to have a tough job proving their worth. And it would be my job to convince teachers they could benefit from working with a coach, no matter how long or deep their own experience. But, I never imagined how difficult my new colleagues' journey would be.

During the first year, I found myself coaching my coaches. I served as a thought partner, resource provider, mentor, and cheerleader while the coaches focused on building relationships with individual teachers and teams. This was not an easy task, first, because the coaches divided their time between two campuses. Second, teacher planning with the coaches was not mandatory and few structures were in place to help coaches affect teaching and learning.

The coaches put out a "get-to-know-you" survey to learn teachers' needs, but they received a low response rate. They ate in the teacher's lounge to have personal, casual conversations, but weren't always welcomed. The "establishing-trusting-relationships" stage of coaching was taking longer than usual and delaying the learning work of coaching. The coaches and I met every other week to check progress. I suggested ways to get their foot in the door, such as sharing a strong resource for a lesson they knew a team would soon be teaching.

Then, at the start of the second semester, our principal asked teachers to meet with the coaches during Tuesday planning sessions. Some teams still resisted. I heard statements like, "Why do we have to meet with the coaches?" On Tuesdays, the coaches would be met at the door by some teams who let them know that, "We are good," and didn't need to meet with them. I promoted the coaches when I sat in on team meetings. If teachers mentioned they weren't as comfortable teaching reading, I would recommend asking the ELA coach to model a lesson in their classroom. The best part of these conversations was seeing when teams did contact a coach. Of course, the innovators latched on first to utilize the coaches as a resource. And, as word spread that the coaches really knew their content and pedagogy, teachers began to reach out. Our ELA coach was able to complete the entire coaching process — co-planning, modeling, and debriefing a reading lesson. The teacher recorded the session and shared it with her team because they had just started a new reading curriculum and benefitted from seeing it in practice.

While there were bright spots throughout the two years, many days left the coaches so discouraged they pleaded to return to their own classrooms. On those days I mentored them about the importance of celebrating "small wins," especially on our veteran-heavy campus. I reminded them that the math/science coach had gained a HUGE victory when a teacher asked her to teach the team about rekenreks. Such manipulatives are not something we use much on our campus, and a team was willing to try because they had the coach's support. Celebrating these wins was important!

When we compared Years 1 and 2 of teacher survey results, we knew our coaches were deepening trust and shifting practice. Throughout Year 2, teachers were more willing to plan with coaches, approach them for new instructional strategies, and value them as a resource. I called these shifts a "big win" for a campus that started from such a strong anti-coaching stance.

— *Leslie Ceballos*

Assistant Principal Leslie Ceballos (left, front) facilitates a teacher learning team.

CHAPTER 6

For example, a principal works with a social studies team that is in the first year of implementing new instructional materials. She observes the team in a goal-setting session for an upcoming unit. Based on the discussion, she hypothesizes the team has not yet deeply invested in the new materials. While some team members reference the new materials, there is little evidence in the conversation that they understand the curriculum thoroughly enough to identify possible reasons for student performance on recent assessments to determine where to focus next. The principal proposes that the team revisit their learning cycle and spend more time in Stage 1 Analyze data. The principal requests that everyone bring student work from the current unit because it might provide an opportunity to discuss gaps between what students understand and what the curriculum explores. She thinks that if the team examines this gap, they may develop greater clarity about the content of the materials as well as the learning needs of the students and members of the learning team. Throughout this and subsequent conversations, the principal may use a consultative stance and different facilitation skills to get the team back on track.

Learning principals know the importance of supporting and monitoring the progress of their teams. In addition to providing just-in-time coaching as teams meet, they set annual calendars to protect team time and meetings with team leads. In large schools, where there are several assistant principals, the leadership team works together through the same strategies to keep all teams moving through the cycle several times throughout the year. With their calendars, charts of each team, and their notes, school leaders host regular leadership learning sessions about how teams are doing, what kind of support teams need, where they are not finding success, and how, as administrators, they can help one other to ensure that all staff members are learning.

Effective coaching can lead to improving team application of the learning cycle or cycle of continuous improvement. While teams may believe they are following the cycle, principal coaching can elicit deeper understanding and appreciation for what the cycle has to offer them. Principals use team minutes along with team lead check-ins to stay informed and they attend team sessions to gain a deeper appreciation and understanding of team commitment and progress.

Learning principals use coaching to develop and share leadership

The principal as coach is intentional about building leaders throughout the school. They invite staff to take the lead in strategic efforts. They know well that by building leadership throughout the school, they are turning the power of choice over to their staff. When staff have the choice to lead, they are more likely to lead with commitment and gratitude rather than compliance or resentment. Principals use a range of leadership strategies, including coaching, in their work with leadership and school improvement teams. They are committed to developing the leadership skills essential to high-quality planning and decision making. These skills require practice and feedback. Principals may set the initial agenda; however, they recognize that over time, even agenda setting can be shared or turned over to others. Moving from leading to distributing leadership requires careful planning, practice, and coaching. Principals as coaches might ask, "What do you and your team really think about that idea?" "Would you be willing to share what you are learning with other teams?" "How do you propose to help others to adopt these ideas?"

The principal adopts the mediating stance during discussions and decision making — asking questions

86 The LEARNING PRINCIPAL

Learning Forward

and posing assumptions that enable the group to grow, think deeply, and make thoughtful decisions. Coaching can be used after decision making to promote reflection and future planning. Through the coaching role, principals help develop individual and team leadership that is essential to achieving schoolwide and team goals.

Principals recognize the importance of helping all teams see how they are contributing to the progress of the school. They may use a collaborative stance to facilitate a celebration of learning or progress. Providing relevant data, asking reflective questions, and giving feedback are all coaching strategies that principals may draw from in order to elevate the important accomplishments of individuals and teams. When principals keep pushing and fail to acknowledge progress, teams run out of energy. Principals lift energy when they make it a priority to recognize progress and learning. Through reflective coaching sessions, teams renew their commitment to their own learning, grow more confident as learners, and develop deeper commitment for the learning of all on their team and their students. Authentic celebrations of learning bring new energy to an organization and inspire teachers and teaching teams to give learning their best every time.

Taking action

Effective learning principals transition smoothly between appraiser and coach. Staff members recognize these transitions and embrace and trust the principal in the coach role. Learning principals realize that some staff members may find it difficult to see their principal from this perspective. By building and maintaining trusting relationships, however, and consistently demonstrating traits of wisdom, principals are more likely to persuade staff to accept them as coaches.

1. Provide specific and actionable feedback

A key to a successful appraisal process is the quality of feedback principals share with teachers. Ensuring teachers' access to feedback is essential for learning and growth. Research evidence suggests that teacher growth reaches a plateau after three years absent any opportunities for feedback and direction for growth (Rivkin, Hanushek, & Kain, 2005). Quality feedback leading to improvement is data driven, based on shared definitions and understandings, acts as a foundation for conversation, and includes goals that improve teacher practice (Hirsh, Psencik, & Brown, 2018).

Learning principals engage in professional learning regarding appraisal observation criteria; they learn how to look for fidelity of implementation and how to ensure they offer their feedback in a manner that will have the intended impact. If such learning is not offered by the school system, they find it through other organizations. They strengthen their own professional learning with practice and reflection with other principals. They demonstrate the value they place on feedback by asking for it from their peers and teachers.

Effective feedback is based on clearly defined expected behaviors, acknowledges progress toward expectations, and provides guidance for achieving full implementation. Educators consider and decide what evidence best demonstrates the expected practices and their results. Giving and receiving feedback about successes and improvements requires skillfulness in leveraging clear, nonjudgmental communication based on evidence, commitment to continuous improvement and shared goals, and trusting, respectful relationships between those giving and receiving feedback. Frequent feedback supports continuous improvement, whereas occasional feedback is often considered evaluative. Feedback about progress toward expected practices provides encouragement to sustain the desired changes over time (Archer et al., 2016).

Learning principals provide feedback in both their appraiser and coaching roles. Teachers as well as teams of teachers face numerous challenges every day. Knowing they can approach their principal for support with the challenges without concern for retribution is evident in healthy school climates. Having confidence in their principals' ability to coach them through a process that leads to solutions to their challenges is another hallmark of a learning school.

Ultimately, the value of feedback is measured by the changes it prompts. Effective feedback lays the groundwork for teachers to recognize, accept, and commit to ongoing improvements. Teachers' confidence in their observers and the procedures they use will affect the degree to which teachers embrace feedback as a means to help them improve (Archer et al., 2016). See Tool 6.2: Leveraging Feedback for additional support with engagement in feedback sessions.

2. Hone coaching skills

Effective coaches exhibit high-level skills in listening, observing, and questioning that help their coachees become more thoughtful and reflective. They skillfully guide coachees through a process of understanding the problems they encounter and help them see options to achieve their goals. Successful coaches develop precise skills, including the ability to lead adults to learn, use targeted questioning to help coachees overcome learning barriers, and employ effective strategies that get them to commit to new skills and behaviors. Most important, coaches are skilled in helping coachees set their own goals,

determine conditions of satisfaction, learn new skills to help them achieve those goals, and commit to follow through (Psencik, 2011).

District leaders ensure that principals have adequate and ongoing support to develop and maintain their coaching skills. Learning principals are committed to professional learning. They meet regularly in their own learning communities, just as their teachers meet in learning teams. They delve into data, share issues they are facing, and try new coaching strategies with each other. They may review tapes of coaching sessions so all can reflect on each other's work and offer feedback. As principals learn from each other, simulate coaching sessions, and share their struggles, they further develop their skills and practices, which in turn helps the individuals they are coaching grow.

Learning principals ensure that staff understand their commitment to coaching. In their coaching role, principals ask staff members questions in a way that: fosters self-awareness and awareness of others; helps them practice astute listening; encourages their observations of the world; enables possibility thinking, thoughtful planning, and decision making; champions opportunities and potential; fosters stretch thinking; inspires them to achieve their goals; challenges their perceived limitations in order to illuminate new possibilities; and supports them in creating alternative ways of thinking.

Effective listening skills are a prerequisite to success in the coaching role. When principals are listening from others' perspectives — listening to understand, listening without judgment or obligation to solve the problem or without having to be the expert — they give individuals and teams space to struggle with an issue, experiment with new ideas, and determine their own learning paths. See Tool 6.3: Practicing Committed Listening for practice with that technique. At the heart of coaching lies the development of a natural curiosity so that individuals and teams begin to think in new ways, question current practices, and reflect about the impact of their work on student learning.

3. Set a path for growth based on the features of wisdom

While coaches understand the importance of developing their skills and character, learning coaches also focus on developing wisdom. Character is who a person is. Skills are the technical applications of coaching. Wisdom has to do with the way coaches make decisions in times of great complexity. Wisdom and developing wisdom may seem like an enigma; some may believe wisdom evolves with experience and age. Tu Moonwalker and JoAnne O'Brien-Levin (2008), however, write that wisdom comes from seeking clarity in beliefs, relationships, and values; living with integrity; and continuously seeking access to an inner compass. Those who work to develop in these areas develop wisdom.

Learning principals may begin that journey by identifying wise individuals and consider how those mentors demonstrated the features of wisdom discussed in this chapter. Co-author Kay Psencik (2011) remembers her grandmother as an exemplar of wisdom in practice:

> When I was a small child, I spent many hours with my grandparents. My mom worked, and after school we often found our way up the block for an afternoon visit and a snack in the comfort of my grandmother's loving home. My grandmother was gentle, funny, and loving, and I always wanted to be with her. My grandmother had great wisdom. She accepted others as they were. Though she had high expectations for her children

and grandchildren, she loved and enjoyed us just the way we were. Grandmother believed that as long as she was alive, she was on earth to serve others. Even in her later years in a nursing home, she adopted a young nurse whose family was in desperate need of basic clothing. Because of Grandmother's transparency, I could always predict what she would think of something I did. I can never forget the joy in my grandmother's life and the light in her eyes. She loved a joke or a funny story and laughed often. My grandmother knew who she was and held deep core values about life, family, community, church, and country. My grandmother celebrated my progress and cheered me on whether it was learning to drive a car or pursue my life dreams. (p. 184)

Psencik (2011) describes a wise person as one who has extensive factual and theoretical knowledge, knows how to live well, is successful at living well, and gives hope to others through her life experience. Wise coaches "know themselves, live in lightness, and are clear that they are on a lifelong journey of service to others" (p. 184). According to Psencik, the core components of wisdom are *acceptance, service, self-awareness, persistence, transparency, lightness,* and *hope.* Acceptance is the ability to see others as unique and remain open to their differing points of view, feelings, and thoughts. Seeking to understand and accept others is a precursor to developing positive relationships. Coaches serve when they find ways to lead those they coach in making thoughtful decisions for themselves, modeling what they want to see in the world, and leading others effectively. Through coaching, principals lead others to set audacious goals for themselves and to have the self-confidence to achieve them.

CHAPTER 6

Reflections

- How will I balance my roles as appraiser and coach with teams and individuals?

- How can I develop my capacity further in using coaching stances and coaching skills?

- In what situations can I strive to be perceived as a wise learning leader?

- How can I ensure that staff members receive high-quality feedback that supports their growth and leads us to achieve our schoolwide student learning goals?

- What processes can support me in understanding the impact of the feedback and support I offer on individual and team performance and student growth?

Wise coaches also are self-aware. "Self-awareness," writes, Psencik "is central to emotional intelligence; emotional intelligence is vital to successful leadership" (p. 185). Persistence is the ability to stay engaged in a course of action despite opposition. Effective coaches help educators ignore distractions and stay focused on their goals and commitments. As they do, these coaches also live in transparency and authenticity so that the people they coach can count on them and "grow strong and confident in their presence" (p. 186). Wise coaches help others live in lightness by spreading positive emotions and articulating a dream that elicits optimism and energy. The idea of lightness relates to the necessity of coaches' modeling actions based on hope so that educators can work through challenges with optimism, integrity, and perseverance. Learning and applying additional coaching skills gives principals a powerful array of tools to leverage in their role as coach.

Principals may use Tool 6.4: Capturing Five Insights to Wisdom to reflect deeply on the aspects of wisdom related to the characteristics and actions of an effective principal as coach.

Conclusion

Effective principals are savvy managers, keen appraisers, and continuous learners. School leaders who value their role as lead learner will expand their functions beyond manager to strengthen their "other-centered" coaching skills. In focusing on others' issues, coach principals give educators, instructional coaches, and other campus leaders opportunities to learn and achieve their own goals. By focusing on others, learning principals develop and share leadership through coaching. They hone their listening and questioning skills, which they turn to the service of learning teams and individuals so that those educators can improve the conditions for teaching and learning for all.

References

Archer, J., Cantrell, S., Holtzman, S., Joe, J., Tocci, C., & Wood, J. (2016). *Better feedback for better teaching: A practical guide to improving classroom observations.* Bill & Melinda Gates Foundation. Available at https://k12education.gatesfoundation.org/resource/better-feedback-for-better-teaching-a-practical-guide-to-improving-classroom-observations/

Bryan, C. & Kaylor, B. (2018). Building blocks of collaboration. *The Learning Professional, 39*(6), 54–60.

Hargrove, R. (1995). *Masterful coaching: Extraordinary results by impacting people and the way they think and work together.* Jossey-Bass.

Hirsh, S., Psencik, K., & Brown, F. (2018). *Becoming a learning system* (Revised ed.). Learning Forward.

International Coach Federation (ICF). (n.d.) About ICF. [Website]. Available at https://coachfederation.org/about

Killion, J. (2007, April). Focus on NSDC's standards: Fit the strategy to the learner. *T3: Teachers Teaching Teachers, 2*(7), 5.

Killion, J. & Harrison, C. (2017). *Taking the lead: New roles for teachers and school-based coaches* (2nd ed.). Learning Forward.

Learning Forward. (2011). *Standards for Professional Learning.* Author.

Lipton, L. & Wellman, B. (2001). *Mentoring matters: A practical guide to learning-focused relationships.* MiraVia.

Lipton, L. & Wellman, B. (2007). How to talk so teachers listen. *Education Leadership, 65*(1), 30–34.

Luczak, J., Perkins, A., Frades, K.S., & Morgan, R.L. (2015). *Giving teachers the feedback and support they deserve: Five essential practices.* EducationFirst.

Moonwalker, T. & O'Brien-Levin, J. (2008). *Business revolution through ancestral wisdom.* Outskirts Press.

Psencik, K. (2011). *The coach's craft: Powerful practices to support school leaders.* Learning Forward.

Rivkin, S., Hanushek, E., & Kain, J. (2005). Teachers, schools, and academic achievement. *Econometrica, 73*(2), 417–458.

Tools index for Chapter 6

Tool	Title	Use
6.1	Developing Coaching Skills and Understanding Stances	This tool supports principals in understanding and strengthening essential coaching skills and stances to fulfill learning needs.
6.2	Leveraging Feedback	This tool guides principals in learning to engage with teachers and teaching teams in meaningful conversations about their practice.
6.3	Practicing Committed Listening	This tool helps principals develop their listening skills.
6.4	Capturing Five Insights to Wisdom	This tool helps promote deeper understanding and appreciation of the attributes of wisdom.

CHAPTER 7

Applying high standards to principal learning

Where are we now?

The principal understands the significance of leadership standards and how they inform individual practice and school leadership practice in the school district.

STRONGLY AGREE   AGREE   NO OPINION   DISAGREE   STRONGLY DISAGREE

The principal can describe the alignment between the Professional Standards for Educational Leaders and other standards including InTASC and Standards for Professional Learning.

STRONGLY AGREE   AGREE   NO OPINION   DISAGREE   STRONGLY DISAGREE

The principal is familiar with a variety of professional standards (e.g. content, teaching, assessment) and their connection with the advancement of equity and excellence for all students.

STRONGLY AGREE   AGREE   NO OPINION   DISAGREE   STRONGLY DISAGREE

Professional learning in the school is grounded in Standards for Professional Learning.

STRONGLY AGREE   AGREE   NO OPINION   DISAGREE   STRONGLY DISAGREE

The principal uses all standards to inform her personal growth plan.

STRONGLY AGREE   AGREE   NO OPINION   DISAGREE   STRONGLY DISAGREE

CHAPTER 7

Being a learning principal means that I have the opportunity to learn with other principals and participate in a professional learning community. This activity not only keeps me in the continuous improvement cycle with my own practice but also includes others' practices within my school. Working in community with my peers allows me to try out new learning designs and protocols before implementing them. As a learning principal I know that I am vulnerable in front of staff, so I embrace that vulnerability to show teachers my efforts to improve my practice. I am a learner and I have high expectations for teachers and myself to learn and grow.

Rachel Harris
Principal, Santa Fe High School
Santa Fe ISD
Santa Fe, Texas

Overview

The principal's job is extremely complex. Each day, principals handle hundreds of different tasks and often engage in more than 50 separate interactions in any given hour (Peterson & Cosner, 2005; Peterson & Deal, 1998). As principals manage their intense workload, they are also under scrutiny like never before with high expectations to be the instructional leaders of their buildings (Council of Chief State School Officers, 2015). Professional standards can play a vital role in preparing principals to address all aspects of their positions by informing their learning, decisions, and shifts in practice.

During the last two decades educators have witnessed a proliferation of educational standards. Standards have been developed for almost every aspect of education to create the potential for shared understanding of excellence and to advance how the entire education system serves students. Such standards address content, assessment, leadership, principal supervisors, social emotional learning, personalized learning, professional learning, mentoring, and more. Unless directed to use particular standards, principals have a lot of autonomy in the degree to which standards guide their work. As a rule, standards shine a light on critical topics in schools. Grounded in recent research, they typically outline best practices and codify them into standards to strengthen the consistency of application to benefit all students. While principals may understand the purpose of standards, the day-to-day realities of leading schools challenge them to make the best use of all of the resources available. This chapter provides school leaders with guidance and tools to realize the potential impact of a deeper understanding and investment in standards.

Principals develop peer learning partnership

In August 2017 I was beginning my fourth year as a school principal in a high-Title I elementary with more than 800 K–6th-grade students. With three years of leadership under my belt, I was experienced enough that I no longer was considered new but was not a veteran principal. Yet, I was one of two experienced leaders among the 10 elementary schools that feed into our neighborhood high school. That year we principals were charged as instructional leaders with implementing a new district initiative: standards-based grading.

I saw the leadership within our feeder pattern as an opportunity for collaboration. Entering my fourth year, I realized how lonely the principal role can be. While I had students, parents, and staff to work with all day, I was alone in my own professional development. I read the suggested resources on standards-based grading, alone. I watched the suggested videos on standards-based grading, alone. Soon, I would begin to implement and roll out a professional learning plan, alone. With support from my area superintendent, I reached out to the new leaders in my region. Promising breakfast and collaboration, I invited them to meet on my campus, during the school day, to analyze site data and develop a common plan.

Alas, on the day of the meeting I was sure they would never work with me again. A conflict forced us to crowd into a smaller conference room. Our meeting was interrupted twice, once by an unplanned fire alarm, and again, by an upset kindergartner who opened the door, yelled an obscenity at me, then threw an umbrella. I quickly moved to catch the umbrella and missed. Surely these leaders would not see me as a credible collaborative partner!

But I was wrong.

Four other principals kept learning with me using Google Hangouts. We continued our conversations on standards-based grading and were transparent with achievement data, teacher data, and our respective sites' level of understanding and implementation of current standards. Those online meetings soon morphed into face-to-face meetings, and we began documenting our learning as a principal professional learning community. Allowing ourselves to be vulnerable and transparent with our data was scary at first but became rewarding as we proceeded.

In collaborative conversations supported by research and data analysis, we chose to apply John Hattie's visible learning to drive professional learning for ourselves and our teachers. We worked together to bring in consultants and develop learning designs for our teachers. We brought our five elementary schools together to learn as larger groups. We were transparent with teachers about how we had settled on the work. We also included them in designing and unwrapping our standards, thus creating buy-in among our major stakeholders.

Increasingly, school districts expect teachers to work in professional learning communities, to be transparent with data, self-reflective in their strengths and areas for growth, and possess a mindset that all students are "our students." As principals we must ask, "Do we hold ourselves to the same standards of collaboration and learning?" I have learned that one of the most critical points of leadership is to allow myself to be vulnerable and open to new learning. If I consider myself to be the lead learner on my campus, I need to model collaborative professional learning with my peers. The vision at my school is, "What starts here, changes a community." I hold to that vision daily because I know that creating and sustaining lifelong learners in our community starts with me.

— *Christel Swinehart-Arbogast*

CHAPTER 7

The influence of leadership standards

In 1996, the Interstate School Leaders Licensure Consortium (ISLLC) released the first Standards for School Leaders. Their release was a powerful moment in the field of education leadership. The ISLLC Principles helped make the case for standards as a key lever for improving education leadership and results for students:

- Standards should reflect the centrality of student learning.
- Standards should acknowledge the changing role of the school leader.
- Standards should recognize the collaborative nature of school leadership.
- Standards should inform performance-based systems of assessment and evaluation of school leaders.
- Standards should be integrated and coherent.
- Standards should be predicated on the concepts of access, opportunity, and empowerment for all members of the school community.

In 2008, the ISLLC standards were refined to reflect new research on leadership, including the seminal report, *How Leadership Influences Student Learning*. That report alerted the field that among all school-related factors, leadership is second only to classroom instruction in influencing student outcomes (Leithwood et al., 2004).

In 2015, the National Policy Board for Educational Administration (NPBEA) introduced the Professional Standards for Educational Leaders, the next generation of ISLLC standards. Once again, new research and a deepening understanding of leadership practice as well as greater consensus in the field regarding the role of principals helped inform these new standards. The new standards took a strong position on the leader's role in improving results for students.

The 2015 Standards have been recast with a stronger, clearer emphasis on students and student learning, outlining foundational principles of leadership to help ensure that each child is well-educated and prepared for the 21st century. For (student) learning to happen, educational leaders must pursue all realms of their work with an unwavering attention to students. They must approach every teacher evaluation, every interaction with central office, every analysis of data with one question always in mind: How will this help our students excel as learners? (NPBEA, 2015, pp. 2–3)

As of this writing, according to the Education Commission of the States, 50 states and the District of Columbia have adopted or adapted the voluntary, nationally recognized leadership standards, with 20 having directly adopted, or working to adopt, the 2015 Professional Standards for Educational Leaders (http://ecs.force.com/mbdata/MBQuest2RTANW?rep=SLC1801). Principals have a responsibility to learn whether their state is among those who have adopted the Standards or have pending legislation that could influence expectations for them.

In its introduction to the standards for educational leaders, the National Policy Board of Educational Administrators (2015) argues that the model professional standards are meant to "communicate expectations to practitioners, supporting institutions, professional associations, policy makers, and the public about the work, qualities, and values of effective educational leaders" (p. 4). It was assumed districts would use these standards, or an adapted form adopted by their states, to paint a picture of the expectations for and work of principals throughout their respective systems (see Table 7.1 on page 97).

APPLYING HIGH STANDARDS TO PRINCIPAL LEARNING

Table 7.1: Standards Function as an Interdependent System for Student Learning

Professional Standards for Educational Leaders	Driver standards — Foundational standards	Core standards — Main business of teaching and learning	Support standards — Professional learning, resources, community, infrastructure
Standard 1. Mission, Vision, and Core Values Effective educational leaders develop, advocate, and enact a shared mission, vision, and core values of high-quality education and academic success and well-being of each student.	■		
Standard 2. Ethics and Professional Norms Effective educational leaders act ethically and according to professional norms to promote each student's academic success and well-being.	■		
Standard 3. Equity and Cultural Responsiveness Effective educational leaders strive for equity of educational opportunity and culturally responsive practices to promote each student's academic success and well-being.	■		
Standard 4. Curriculum, Instruction, and Assessment Effective educational leaders develop and support intellectually rigorous and coherent systems of curriculum, instruction, and assessment to promote each student's academic success and well-being.		■	
Standard 5. Community of Care and Support for Students Effective educational leaders cultivate an inclusive, caring, and supportive school community that promotes the academic success and well-being of each student.		■	
Standard 6. Professional Capacity of School Personnel Effective educational leaders develop the professional capacity and practice of school personnel to promote each student's academic success and well-being.			■
Standard 7. Professional Community for Teachers and Staff Effective educational leaders foster a professional community of teachers and other professional staff to promote each student's academic success and well-being.			■
Standard 8. Meaningful Engagement of Families and Community Effective educational leaders engage families and the community in meaningful, reciprocal, and mutually beneficial ways to promote each student's academic success and well-being.			■
Standard 9. Operations and Management Effective educational leaders manage school operations and resources to promote each student's academic success and well-being.			■
Standard 10. School Improvement Effective educational leaders act as agents of continuous improvement to promote each student's academic success and well-being.	■		

www.learningforward.org

Each standard statement begins with the words "Effective educational leaders" and ends with a version of the phrase "academic success and well-being of each student." All ten standards demonstrate a clear link between the actions of the building principal and results for each student. Each standard emphasizes the responsibility of principals for creating the supporting conditions that lead to children's academic success and well-being. Each educational leadership standard is then followed by the elements that outline the work that is needed for an effective leader to actualize the standard successfully.

The National Policy Board (Wilson, 2018) organizes standards into three clusters: drivers, core, and supports. **Driver** standards are foundational and help the principal drive the organization:

- Mission, Vision, and Core Values [S1]
- Ethics and Professional Norms [S2]
- Equity and Cultural Responsiveness [S3]
- School Improvement [S10]

Core standards get to the heart of why principals are engaged in this work. They represent the primary business of schools: supporting academic results and well-being for students. They also shine a spotlight on the job of principal as instructional leader. The following are considered core standards:

- Curriculum, Instructional, and Assessment [S4]
- Community of Care and Support for Students [S5]

Finally, **support** standards highlight the fact that principals are one step removed from interacting directly with teaching and learning. They, however, directly support those who do. If principals are to be "multipliers of effective teaching and leadership practices" (Manna, 2015, p. 7), they support the ongoing growth and development of others. They also engage families and the community to bring more resources and assistance to their students. Finally, they ensure the building is running smoothly so there are no barriers to the core work of schools. The following are support standards:

- Professional Capacity of School Personnel [S6]
- Professional Community for Teachers and Staff [S7]
- Meaningful Engagement of Families and Community [S8]
- Operations and Management [S9]

The Professional Standards for Educational Leaders and the ISLLC Standards that preceded them have influenced district policy and procedures in various ways. One district, Ft. Wayne (Indiana) Community Schools, used national leadership standards to inform a systemwide definition of leadership. The district felt a leadership definition would serve as a foundation for a deeper exploration of leadership expectations and practices:

Leaders, through disciplined thoughts and actions, create and sustain the conditions that ensure achievement of our moral purpose by:

- Shaping a shared vision and commitment to action for academic and social success for all students;
- Developing systems that support students and adults;
- Modeling and cultivating courageous leadership;
- Distributing responsibility for people, data, and processes that nurtures a culture of continuous improvement and empowerment (Hirsh et al., 2018).

Denver (Colorado) Public Schools is another district that adopted or adapted a complete set of leadership standards informed by national standards. Denver was a participating district in The Wallace Foundation's Principal Pipeline Initiative discussed in Chapter 8. The district's School Leadership Framework highlights expectations for school leaders and "sets the foundation for recruitment, selection, leadership preparation, performance reviews, professional growth, and succession planning" (p. x).

While the Professional Standards for Educational Leaders provide guidance for leadership in the United States, other countries and regions have similar standards in place. Like the Council of Chief State School Officers and National Policy Board for Educational Administrators in the U.S., the Australian Institute for Teaching and School Leadership adopted the Principal Standard to guide aspiring and current principals on what they need to know and do to succeed as school leaders. The Australian standard for principals is divided into leadership requirements and professional practices. For example, "vision and values" represents a leadership requirement and "developing self and others" is a professional practice.

School leaders in Australia can use the Australian Professional Standard for Principals at various stages in their careers to support their development and ongoing growth. The Australian model identifies three key leadership requirements followed by five key professional practices needed to enact the requirements (see Figure 7.1 on page 100).

Intersection of professional educational leadership standards and other professional standards

For the most part, professional standards have been developed independent of each other. Such discontinuity creates challenges for principals who try to integrate standards into their daily work. Many principals may pick and choose which standard seems most relevant and helpful at the time they are reading them. Learning principals take a more methodical

---

Example Principal Standards (Denver Public Schools)

Principal

Instructional Expertise. Builds, develops, and empowers the school's Instructional Leadership Team to ensure all students engage in joyful, rigorous, and personalized learning and demonstrate high academic achievement

Vision & Strategy. Drives a schoolwide compelling vision of equity through strategic planning, change leadership and school improvement, and innovative practices

People & Culture. Recruits, selects, retains, and grows a highly effective leadership team and staff, developing a culture of continuous learning that maximizes staff and student morale and performance

Community & Equity. Leads a positive, inclusive school community that supports the development of the Whole Child and meaningfully engages students, families, and community members

Personal & Values. Inspires others through values-driven, reflective, and resilient leadership

Operational & Organizational. Achieves school goals by driving results, maximizing resources, and ensuring effective management of school systems and operations

Source: 2017 School Leadership Framework, Denver City Public Schools (http://thecommons.dpsk12.org/cms/lib/CO01900837/Centricity/Domain/110/Lead%20in%20Denver/School%20Leadership%20Framework%202017.pdf)

CHAPTER 7

Figure 7.1: Example of Australian Standard Framework

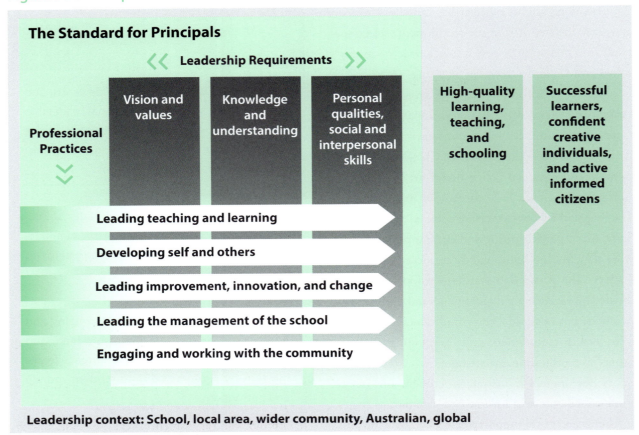

Source: Reprinted from *Australian Professional Standard for Principals and the Leadership Profiles,* p. 10. Copyright 2019 Education Services Australia.

approach to integrating standards into their school improvement and individual learning plans. This section explores some examples of the relationships between the Professional Standards for Educational Leaders (NPBEA, 2015) and other standards as well as how principals may use this information to guide their decisions and practice.

Chapter 1 discusses how the driving force for the learning principal mission and vision is equity and excellence. This book also discusses how learning principals hold high expectations and provide essential support to help students meet rigorous academic standards. All three of these core concepts are represented in the core standards for curriculum and instruction of the Professional Standards for Educational Leaders (see Table 7.2 on page 101).

Although principals are not in classrooms teaching each day, their actions help create the conditions for effective teaching and learning. Standard 4 of the Professional Standards for Educational Leaders focuses on the work principals do to support curriculum, instruction, and assessment. It reads:

Effective educational leaders develop and support intellectually rigorous and coherent

APPLYING HIGH STANDARDS TO PRINCIPAL LEARNING

Table 7.2: Core Work of the Learning Principal Aligns With the Professional Standards for Educational Leaders

Concepts	Standards
Equity and excellence	**Standard 3. Equity and Cultural Responsiveness** Effective educational leaders strive for equity of educational opportunity and culturally responsive practices to promote each student's academic success and well-being
High expectations	**Standard 4. Curriculum, Instruction, and Assessment** Effective educational leaders develop and support intellectually rigorous and coherent systems of curriculum, instruction, and assessment to promote each student's academic success and well-being
Essential [student] support to meet academic standards	**Standard 5. Community of Care and Support for Students** Effective educational leaders cultivate an inclusive, caring, and supportive school community that promotes the academic success and well-being of each student.

systems of curriculum, instruction, and assessment to promote each student's academic success and well-being. (NPBEA, 2015, p. 12) The elements for this standard include:

1. Implement coherent systems of curriculum, instruction, and assessment that promote the mission, vision, and core values of the school, embody high expectations for student learning, align with academic standards, and are culturally responsive.

2. Align and focus systems of curriculum, instruction, and assessment within and across grade levels to promote student academic success, love of learning, the identities and habits of learners, and healthy sense of self.

3. Promote instructional practice that is consistent with knowledge of child learning and development, effective pedagogy, and the needs of each student.

4. Ensure instructional practice that is intellectually challenging, authentic to student experiences, recognizes student strengths, and is differentiated and personalized.

5. Promote the effective use of technology in the service of teaching and learning.

6. Employ valid assessments that are consistent with knowledge of child learning and development and technical standards of measurement.

7. Use assessment data appropriately and within technical limitations to monitor student progress and improve instruction. (p. 12)

The elements provide further explanation of the particular actions the learning principal will take to meet the standard and achieve the mission. Further support for these concepts can be found in other professional standards documents. In order to be successful actualizing the first element, "Align with academic standards," the principal must have deep knowledge of the college- and career-ready standards to which students will be held accountable for mastering. "Academic standards are a promise of equity," according to Student Achievement Partners

www.learningforward.org

The LEARNING PRINCIPAL **101**

CHAPTER 7

(https://achievethecore.org/), a nonprofit dedicated to improving student achievement. The site goes on to describe the ideal situation for every student as follows:

- When every student is expected to learn rich content and is supported every day in doing so from kindergarten to high school graduation, we deliver on that promise.

- We believe that a transformative education is not a luxury reserved for only some. We believe that educating every single student in the richly complex disciplines of literacy and mathematics not only safeguards democracy, but cultivates it further.

- This is not the current reality for most students. And a devastating amount of evidence tells us the distance between vision and reality is even greater for students who live in poverty or are of color. We are convinced there is much work still to do. (What We Believe, para. 1–3)

Principals need not only a commitment to rigorous academic standards, but also a deep understanding of literacy and mathematics standards, in particular. Learning principals engage in deep study and learning experiences that develop the level of understanding necessary for their role. They invest in their state academic standards as well as the various content standards that preceded their development (e.g., National Council of Teachers of Mathematics standards for mathematics, National Council of Teachers of English/International Literacy Association standards for literacy). The 2019 literacy leadership brief titled *Principals as Literacy Leaders* states, "If we truly believe every child has a basic human right to read, principals have a moral imperative to monitor and ensure equitable practices that nurture students' self-efficacy and lead to comparable academic outcomes" (p. 2).

A second example of the interrelationship between the Professional Standards for Educational Leaders (NPBEA, 2015) and other professional standards is evident in Standard 6 focused on teaching and learning: "Effective educational leaders develop the professional capacity and practice of school personnel to promote each student's academic success and well-being" (p. 14).

To actualize many of the elements within this standard, the principal will need a deep understanding of effective teaching practice as outlined by standards such as the Interstate Teacher Assessment and Support Consortium (InTASC) Model Core Teaching Standards and Learning Progressions for Teachers (CCSSO, 2013). According to Council of Chief State School Officers (CCSSO), the teaching standards and learning progressions "describe the new vision of teaching needed for today's learners, how teaching practice that is aligned to the new vision develops over time, and what strategies teachers can employ to improve their practice both individually and collectively" (p. 3).

Principals also have a responsibility to be well-versed in the teaching standards or models of effective practice that have been adopted by their districts. All of these models have roots in several of the professional standards. For example, many districts use the Charlotte Danielson (https://danielsongroup.org/framework) framework while others use models by Robert Marzano (https://www.marzanoresources.com/hrs/high-reliability-schools) or Jon Saphier (http://skillfulteacher.com/). As principals support teaching and learning, having a deep understanding of the model of practice is important so that they can conduct aligned performance reviews and formal evaluations of teaching practice.

Standards guide capacity building for self and others

Learning Forward holds that the professional learning standards are equally essential to every principal committed to the goals of equity and excellence. While the Professional Standards for Educational Leaders lay out a course of action for the school leader, Learning Forward's (2011) Standards for Professional Learning set the agenda for continuous learning and improvement for everyone in the school. No one knows better than the principal that everyone embraces the role of learner if a school is to be successful. While the standards for educational leaders are intended for use by principals and those who support them, Standards for Professional Learning are meant to be shared and used by the principal and those she supports. The seven professional learning standards establish and describe the conditions, processes, and outcomes essential to achieving professional learning's potential. They establish a shared language as well as expectations. Professional learning standards make explicit that the purpose of professional learning is for educators to develop the knowledge, skills, practices, and dispositions they need to help students perform at higher levels. The standards are not a prescription for how education leaders and public officials should address all the challenges related to improving the performance of educators and their students. Instead, the standards focus on one critical issue — professional learning (Learning Forward, 2011).

The Outcome standard emphasizes the purpose of professional learning: "Professional learning that increases educator effectiveness and results for all students aligns its outcomes with educator performance and student curriculum standards" (Learning Forward, 2011, p. 23). It calls on educators to recognize the critical connection between professional learning and

professional standards. The other six standards outline the necessary components of high-quality professional learning. Learning principals understand that they have particular responsibilities as leaders of others, partners in professional learning planning and implementation, and learners themselves through each of the six remaining standards: Learning Communities, Leadership, Resources, Data, Learning Designs, and Implementation.

The Leadership standard provides more details regarding the role and responsibility of principals as well as district and teacher leaders in advancing the learning agenda that leads to achieving a school's mission: "Professional learning that increases educator effectiveness and results for all students requires skillful leaders who develop capacity, advocate, and create support systems for professional learning" (Learning Forward, 2011, p. 23). This standard details key expectations of leaders. First and foremost, they develop capacity for learning and leading by setting the agenda for professional learning and aligning it with classroom, school, and district goals for student and educator learning. Learning leaders serve as vocal advocates for professional learning. They clearly articulate the critical link between increased student learning and educator professional learning. Learning leaders create the structures and support systems essential for all to engage in effective professional learning. They equitably distribute resources to accomplish individual, team, school, and school system goals. They also actively engage policy makers and decision makers so that resources, policies, annual calendars, daily schedules, and structures support professional learning to increase results for students (Learning Forward, 2011).

Considerable overlap exists between Learning Forward's Leadership standard and Standard 7 of the Professional Standard for Educational Leaders

CHAPTER 7

(see sidebar), which is considered the professional learning standard among those standards.

Learning principals, however, recognize the importance of developing among all staff deeper expertise for and commitment to continuous improvement. Principals may apply the Professional Standards for Educational Leaders (NPBEA, 2015) to their own growth plans and the Learning Forward (2011) Standards for Professional Learning to their collective school plans. While the educational leaders standards elements guide the principal, the Standards for Professional Learning offer the depth and clarity principals need to effectively create a strong system of professional learning in their schools. Principals can use Learning Forward's standards to better understand their specific roles in supporting effective systems of professional learning in their schools and districts.

> ### Key Similarities: Two Leadership Standards
>
> **Professional Standards for Educational Leaders**
>
> **Standard 7. Professional Community for Teachers and Staff**
> Effective educational leaders *foster a professional community of teachers and other professional staff* to promote each student's academic success and well-being. (NPBEA, p.15)
>
> **Standards for Professional Learning**
>
> **Leadership standard**
> Professional learning that increases educator effectiveness and results for *all* students *requires skillful leaders who develop capacity, advocate, and create support systems for professional learning.* (Learning Forward, 2011, p. 23)

Taking action

This chapter lays a foundation from which principals can build their understanding about how to apply standards to their leadership practices. It also provides school leaders with guidance and tools to strengthen the impact from an investment in standards by assessing needs, creating learning agendas for their own learning and that of the school, and creating coherence among the standards guiding teaching and learning within schools and across the district.

1. Conduct needs assessments

Learning principals individually assess their strengths and growth areas using a reflective assessment aligned with the educational leadership standards. The previous section provides an overview of the various standards that inform the work of principals, starting with the Professional Standards for Educational Leaders. For example, principals consider completing a self-assessment of their individual practice using rubrics designed by their own or other districts or states. The Maryland Department of Education, through funding from the Southern Regional Education Board, designed its own standards for educational leadership rubric to help principals gather data on their own learning gaps and plan professional learning experiences. Table 7.3 shows an excerpt from the Maryland rubric (see page 105).

The self-assessment leads to the identification of growth areas as well as data to support development of a personal learning agenda. See Tool 7.1: Conducting a Self-Assessment of Leadership Practices.

While assessing their own performance using Professional Standards for Educational Leaders (NPBEA, 2015) is important, learning principals recognize that it

APPLYING HIGH STANDARDS TO PRINCIPAL LEARNING

is equally important to access and monitor data on the degree to which their respective school meets the Standards for Professional Learning (Learning Forward, 2011). Those data can be analyzed and discussed with key leaders within and outside the school to determine appropriate courses of action for supporting school improvement. Just as principals can use Professional Standards for Educational Leaders to identify individual growth areas, the entire staff will benefit from understanding the Standards for Professional Learning

to support changes to the school improvement plan that may be necessitated by the survey results. Tool 7.2: Assessing Quality of Professional Learning gives principals a quick and easy way to gather initial data on the state of professional learning in the school. A more robust, sophisticated tool, the Standards Assessment Inventory (https://consulting.learningforward.org/consulting-services/standards-assessment-inventory/) is available through Learning Forward and can be used to report changes over time.

Table 7.3: Professional Standards for Educational Leaders Rubric

Standard 1. Mission, Vision, and Core Values
Effective educational leaders develop, advocate, and enact a shared mission, vision, and core values of high-quality education and academic success and well-being of each student.

An Ineffective School Leader...	A Developing School Leader...	An Effective School Leader...	A Highly Effective School Leader...
Inconsistently… • Develops and communicates the school's vision, mission, and core values. • Uses data to inform continuous improvement that promotes the success of each student.	• Communicates the school vision, mission, and core values to stakeholders (e.g. parents, teachers, community members). • Facilitates opportunities for stakeholders to collaborate to promote student success.	…reaches the "developing" level and… • Collaboratively develops and implements a student-centered mission and vision that are aligned with the school system's mission and vision. • Uses data and input from stakeholders to inform the development of a mission and vision that promotes effective organizational practices, high-quality education, and academic success for each student.	…reaches and maintains the effective level and… • Provides evidence that stakeholder groups advocate for and is supportive of the school's vision, mission, and core values. • Aligns partnership (e.g. community organizations, vendors) to support implementation of vision, mission, and core values.

Source: *Professional Standards for Educational Leaders Rubric,* p. 7. Copyright 2018 Maryland State Department of Education and Community Training and Assistance Center.

2. Develop or refine learning agendas for self and school faculty

Once learning principals complete a self-assessment or use other means to gather data on their own practice, the next move is for them to develop learning agendas to strengthen gap areas for themselves and school staff members. Stephanie Hirsh, Kay Psencik, and Frederick Brown (2018) define a learning agenda as a collection of strategies or designs leaders select in order to ensure that educators can understand and apply practices that improve their own performance and student outcomes. Armed with data from the self-assessment, a sense of teaching and learning based on a review of teacher evaluations and observations, and a clear picture of how teachers in the school perceive professional learning aligned to the Standards for Professional Learning (Learning Forward, 2011), learning principals will be well positioned to determine individual and collective learning goals.

An example is the principal who realizes the growth mindset inherent in Standard 6 of the Professional Standards for Educational Leaders (NPBEA, 2015), which focuses on professional capacity of school personnel. Additionally, if the assessment of practice shows significant growth opportunity for the Leadership standard in the Standards for Professional Learning (Learning Forward, 2011), she has complementary data sets. The data combine to signal to the principal that she deepen her understanding of professional learning to support teacher growth.

3. Create coherence in use of standards

Principals can find it challenging to integrate all leadership standards to achieve equity and excellence. Hirsh et al., (2018) addressed the necessary elements to develop a coherent learning system in districts, including:

- Value adult learning as much as student learning;
- Align adult practices to student learning outcomes;
- Have a collective responsibility to continuous improvement of people and processes throughout the organization;
- Thrive on precise feedback;
- Provide conditions that scale and sustain effective teaching and leading;
- Commit to innovating;
- Celebrate and honor success. (p. 20)

There is no road map to guide them on this journey. Authentic integration will require principals to create their own road maps with their leadership teams or other principals and supervisors. The process could include identifying and studying standards, recognizing which standards are legislated (in original or adapted forms) and which standards are resources, and then aligning the appropriate standards to school goals and improvement plans. Displaying and discussing their plan to leverage guidance from standards with all stakeholders will instill confidence in the plan as well as the tools selected to support its outcomes. See Tool 7.3: Mapping Standards and Building Coherence to support alignment and coherence.

Conclusion

Learning principals know that each resource is precious, and they recognize that each move they take merits considerable scrutiny. Using the standards to guide school improvement helps standards validate principals' decisions and strengthens their credibility. As a professional field, organizations have invested billions of dollars in research about what works best to help adults and students learn at high levels. Learning principals recognize the power of that investment and use the findings to guide their plans.

Reflections

- How much of our current improvement agenda is based in professional standards?

- How can I be more intentional in using Professional Standards for Educational Leaders, Standards for Professional Learning, and other professional standards to grow professionally?

- How can I be more intentional in using Professional Standards for Educational Leaders, Standards for Professional Learning, and other professional standards to advance our school mission?

- How will my next learning agenda reflect my new understanding of various professional standards for leaders?

- What process will our faculty use to build understanding and appreciation for professional standards?

As principals navigate the various standards that guide their work (e.g. Professional Standards for Educational Leaders, college- and career-ready standards, Standards for Professional Learning, Interstate Teacher Assessment and Support Consortium standards), they are building a learning community that shares collective responsibility for equity and excellence represented in their unique school mission statements.

References

Australian Institute for Teaching and School Leadership (AITSL). (2017). Leading the way for future leaders. [Website]. Available at https://www.aitsl.edu.au/lead-develop/understand-the-principal-standard/how-the-principal-standard-was-developed

Council of Chief State School Officers. (2008). *Educational leadership policy standards.* Author.

Council of Chief State School Officers. (2015). *Model principal supervisor professional standards.* Author.

Council of Chief State School Officers. (2013). *Interstate Teacher Assessment and Support Consortium (INTASC) Model core teaching standards and learning progressions for teachers 1.0: A Resource for ongoing teacher development.* Author. Available at https://ccsso.org/sites/default/files/2017-12/2013_INTASC_Learning_Progressions_for_Teachers.pdf

Denver Public Schools. (2017). *School leadership framework.* Author.

Hirsh, S., Psencik, K., & Brown, F. (2018). *Becoming a learning system.* Learning Forward.

International Literacy Association. (2019). *Literacy leadership brief: Principals as literacy leaders.* Author. Available at https://literacyworldwide.org/docs/default-source/where-we-stand/ila-principals-as-literacy-leaders.pdf

Learning Forward. (2011). *Standards for Professional Learning.* Author.

Leithwood, K., Seashore-Louis, K., Anderson, S., & Wahlstrom, K. (2004). *How leadership influences student learning.* The Wallace Foundation. Available at https://www.wallacefoundation.org/knowledge-center/pages/how-leadership-influences-student-learning.aspx

Manna, P. (2015). *Developing excellent school principals to advance teaching and learning: Considerations for state policy.* The Wallace Foundation. Available at https://www.wallacefoundation.org/ knowledge-center/Documents/Developing-Excellent-School-Principals.pdf

Maryland State Department of Education. (2018, July). *Professional Standards for Educational Leaders rubric.* Maryland State Department of Education (MSDE) and Community Training and Assistance Center (CTAC).

Murphy, J. (2005). Unpacking the foundations of ISLLC Standards and addressing concerns in the academic community. *Educational Administration Quarterly, 41*(154), 166–168.

National Policy Board for Educational Administration (NPBEA) (2015). *Professional Standards for Educational Leaders.* Author.

Peterson, K. & Cosner, S. (2005, Spring). Teaching your principal: Top tips for the professional development of the school's chief. *JSD, 26*(2), 28–32.

Peterson, K. & Deal, T. (1998). How leaders influence the culture of schools, *Educational Leadership, 56*(1), 28–30.

Student Achievement Partners. (n.d.). What We Believe. In *About Us.* [Website]. Available at https://achievethecore.org/about-us

Wilson, J. (2018, September). National Policy Board for Educational Administration. [PowerPoint slides]. Council of Chief State School Officers. Available at http://www.npbea.org/wp-content/uploads/2018/10/NPBEA-Presentaion-to-CCSSO-TLLC-Sept2018.pdf

Tools index for Chapter 7

Tool	Title	Use
7.1	Conducting a Self-Assessment of Leadership Practices	This tool guides individual principals in conducting a self-assessment of their leadership practices as aligned to the Professional Standards for Educational Leaders.
7.2	Assessing Quality of Professional Learning	This tool helps principals gather information on the quality and level of implementation of the Standards for Professional Learning in their schools.
7.3	Mapping Standards and Building Coherence	This tools helps principals strengthen alignment and coherence among the Professional Standards for Educational Leaders and other key standards.

CHAPTER
8

Partnering with central offices to support principals

Where are we now?

The school system has a formal process in place to identify and support the development of a pool of potential principals.

STRONGLY AGREE   AGREE   NO OPINION   DISAGREE   STRONGLY DISAGREE

The school system has relationships with preservice providers, including universities, to ensure their graduates are prepared to lead its schools.

STRONGLY AGREE   AGREE   NO OPINION   DISAGREE   STRONGLY DISAGREE

The school system tracks data on leaders' professional learning, competencies, and professional experiences.

STRONGLY AGREE   AGREE   NO OPINION   DISAGREE   STRONGLY DISAGREE

The school system ensures that principals have access to high-quality individual and team learning experiences.

STRONGLY AGREE   AGREE   NO OPINION   DISAGREE   STRONGLY DISAGREE

The school system designates principal supervisors and assigns each of them a reasonable number of principals to manage.

STRONGLY AGREE   AGREE   NO OPINION   DISAGREE   STRONGLY DISAGREE

CHAPTER 8

> *Our district often refers to a popular John Maxwell quote which states, "Everything rises and falls on leadership." Administrators must model the vulnerability and resilience needed to tend to both the organizational management component, which keeps a building safe and secure, and the instructional component, which supports improved achievement for all students. Although each component is important, our core business must remain teaching and learning. I have served various roles within the district; the one in which I found the greatest success is that of lead learner.*

> Leilani Esmond
> Director of Staff Development
> Gwinnett County Public Schools
> Gwinnett County Board of Education
> Gwinnett County, Georgia

Overview

Chapters 1 through 6 focus on the work that principals undertake individually and with their leadership teams and faculties in school buildings every day. Chapter 7 transitions the perspective from school-based activities to the broader aspect of high-quality standards affecting principal behaviors. This chapter examines the role of the central office, or school district, and its responsibility to establish and sustain conditions that support school leaders throughout the aspiring to retiring moments in their careers.

System leaders cannot leave leadership to chance; they must take an active role in tapping, preparing, placing, supporting, and evaluating local leaders. These priorities are not inconsequential. Efforts to improve principal recruitment, training, evaluation and ongoing development "should be considered highly cost-effective approaches to successful school improvement" (Leithwood et al., 2004, p. 14).

Preparation is key to a great start

Linda Darling-Hammond (2007) led a Wallace Foundation-commissioned study on school leadership titled *Preparing School Leaders for a Changing World: Lessons from Exemplary Leadership Development Programs*. Among many important issues, it addressed the following questions:

- What are the components of programs that provide effective initial preparation and ongoing professional development for principals?
- What qualities and design principles are evident in these exemplary programs?
- Do graduates of exemplary programs demonstrate instructional and organizational leadership practices that are distinctive and that are associated with more effective schools?

The results of the study defined a pivot point in the evolution of leadership preparation by exposing the fact that many programs were not meeting the needs of participants or school districts. Many traditional programs, the study argued, were "out of touch with the real-world complexities and demands of school leadership" (p. 5). The study elevated the importance of providing a meaningful internship experience. In all, the study highlighted the following features as important:

1. Clear focus and values about leadership and learning around which the program is coherently organized;

2. Standards-based curriculum emphasizing instructional leadership, organizational development, and change management;

3. Field-based internships with skilled supervision;

4. Cohort groups that create opportunities for collaboration and teamwork in practice-oriented situations;

5. Active instructional strategies that link theory and practice, such as problem-based learning;

6. Rigorous recruitment and selection of both candidates and faculty;

7. Strong partnerships with schools and districts to support quality, field-based learning.

Jacquelyn Davis (2016) shared the following observations associated with principal preparation:

• District leaders are largely dissatisfied with the quality of principal preparation programs, and many universities believe their programs have room for improvement.

• The course of study at preparation programs does not always reflect principals' real jobs.

• Some university policies and practices can hinder change.

• States have authority to play a role in improving principal preparation, but many are not using this power as effectively as possible.

Learning principals are lifelong learners who appreciate the knowledge inherent in developing their own practice through authentic professional learning. They understand that the more time they spend on intentionality, the more they strengthen their own practice. Learning principals further their practice through reflection, reciprocal coaching and feedback, and a relentless focus on improvement.

Learning principals also realize that their practice correlates with improvement efforts of the school community. For that reason they cherish dual responsibilities: to learn continuously and to improve the lives of those they serve — from the community at large to the student in every seat.

Douglas W. Anthony
Chief Consultant, Anthony Consulting Group
Bowie Maryland

Former Associate Superintendent
Prince George's County Public Schools
Upper Marlboro, Maryland

District evolves and chooses the "right stuff" to develop learning principals

About 10 years ago, I transitioned from my role as elementary school principal to director of school leadership for a large urban school district. Because I'd just left the schoolhouse, I could readily articulate what wasn't working in many of the programs that I was now tasked with supervising. Central office administrators, were working on "stuff" — well-intended stuff — but not necessarily the right stuff to move an individual's practice. I realized that two critical variances existed between **what works** for school leaders in schools and what central office people **think works** for school leaders: (1) The practicality and authenticity of supports and professional learning provided by the central office don't always align with the immediate needs of the school leaders, and (2) given realities in the business of running a school, supports have to take place in real time.

Collaborating with other central service providers across the district to better meet the needs of principals, I learned that three critical elements resolve the disconnect that often exists between school leader needs and central office support. First, a central office has to have a coherent approach to establishing a culture of continuous improvement. Second, a central office has to understand the strategic balance of providing professional learning experiences that meet both the individual and collective needs of the administrators it serves. Third, a central office has to understand how adults learn. Equally important, a central office has to remember that it works in service of the schools and not the reverse.

With a firm understanding of systemic alignment and the value of strategic partnerships within and across the district, we grew smarter by developing a coherence model that framed how we would support schools and their improvement efforts. Then, we took the time to invest in our improvement. Arm in arm with representatives from offices and divisions throughout the district, we launched our improvement effort by crafting a theory of change to anchor our work while providing a common understanding of our cause.

After we adopted a coherence model and theory

Former Principal Doug Anthony meets with colleagues.

of change, we aligned the supports between central office and schools so they were available at times and in sites where leaders most needed them. With that effort, we gained the knowledge that on-the-job, side-by-side coaching and experiential support were paramount in developing leader practice. Secondly, we kept in mind that we were invested in taking a comprehensive approach to leadership development. At that scale we realized the importance of leveraging certain system-wide professional learning experiences, such as coaching, to meet the needs of individual principals while we addressed collective needs across the district. Most importantly, we embraced data from evaluations and aligned our support to the national leader standards that clearly articulate best practices of exceptional leaders. For example, we looked at data about our principals collected from a nationally normed 360-degree evaluation tool. Analyzing those data, we devised professional learning programs based on the aggregate data most applicable to all of our leaders. Principal supervisors, in turn, utilized the individual leader data from that same tool to provide on-the-job, side-by-side coaching support.

This more thoughtful approach, grounded in adult learning theory, moved us from "sit-and-get" to authentic, collaborative, and evidenced-based professional learning.

— *Doug Anthony*

Davis further pointed out that strong university-district partnerships are essential to high-quality preparation but are far from universal. School systems have a responsibility to exercise greater influence over programs that are preparing their leaders. Researchers Margaret Terry Orr, Cheryl King, and Michelle LaPointe (2010) suggest that districts consider three stances for influencing the content and structure of preparation programs that contribute to their principal pipeline: discerning customer, competitor, and collaborator. School systems have greater success with all three stances when they understand and clearly describe the knowledge, skills, and experiences they expect from prospective principal candidates.

According to Orr and colleagues (2010), districts become discerning customers when they are able to articulate their expectations for principal candidates. They can then ask universities and other providers to adjust their programs accordingly. Preparation program providers soon learn that if their graduates aren't meeting district needs, school systems will look elsewhere. In addition, preparation programs could face challenges recruiting candidates for their preparation programs if their graduates are not securing positions in key districts. Still unable to secure the quality or number of principal candidates that they need, districts may decide to develop their own leadership preparation program. Many districts across the country, mostly large urban districts, have launched their own programs including Denver, New York City, and Prince George's County in Maryland. Although some systems require the university-based program as a prerequisite, others do not. That approach is possibly more costly to districts and candidates than others; however, it increases the likelihood candidates will exit the program with a strong sense of the culture and needs of the district (Orr et al., 2010).

Because designing and implementing an internal principal certification program can be costly, many districts may be better served by engaging in special partnerships with universities or other providers. Collaborative efforts are often codified with contracts, scholarships, or acknowledgements of "preferred status" for particular programs. Because districts have worked with these universities and other program providers to ensure the programs are meeting system needs, districts can have a high degree of confidence in the graduates. District personnel may also serve as mentors and adjunct faculty in these programs, so there is even greater alignment. See Tool 8.1: Choosing the Right Partner and Tool 8.2: Clarifying the District-University Partnership for additional guidance with this subject.

From seeking to strengthen their principal development pipelines to ongoing improvement strategies, partnerships with school systems resulted in positive outcomes, including student achievement:

- Outperformance in math for elementary, middle and high school; for reading in elementary and middle school;
- Positive and statistically significant improvement for schools in the lowest quartile of student achievement;
- Benefits to all schools in the systems, not just those with pipeline principals;
- Benefits were seen early in the initiative, beginning in the second year of implementation (Gates et al., 2019).

Such results caused the researchers to report the following: "We found no other comprehensive district-wide initiatives with demonstrated positive effects of this magnitude on achievement" (Gates et al., 2019, p. xx).

Principal supervision is pivotal

When they have sufficient time and well-developed skills to effectively do their work, principal supervisors are a key part of an overall strategy to support principal effectiveness. Especially during a principal's first and second year on the job, the support of a principal supervisor is critical. What districts call their principal supervisors will vary based on size and other contextual factors. In smaller districts, the principal supervisor may be the district superintendent. In other systems, the title may include associate superintendent, chief, director, or network leader. From this point forward, the term *principal supervisor* will be used to describe those who have responsibility for supervising and developing principals.

Over the years interest has grown in examining the impact that principal supervisors can have on principal effectiveness. In their report, Ellen B. Goldring and colleagues (2018) address lessons learned through The Wallace Foundation investment in Broward County, Florida; Baltimore City, Maryland; Cleveland, Ohio; Des Moines, Iowa; Long Beach, California; and Minneapolis, Minnesota. Districts can consider how a principal supervisor might support the principal by reviewing the lessons learned by The Wallace Foundation about the work of these district leaders. The Principal Supervisor Initiative final report showed success in restructuring the principal supervisor position so that it focused on developing and evaluating principals to help them promote effective teaching and learning in their schools. And during the course of the initiative, principals' ratings of their supervisors' effectiveness showed a statistically significant increase. The principals reported greater frequency of supervisor practices that supported development of school leadership, including helping them with data analysis, deepening the quality and frequency of feedback for the principals, and helping them strengthen teacher effectiveness (Goldring et al., 2020). "It's a tremendous change," said a participating principal, "I mean, we're talking goals, we're talking growth, and we're talking data. It's not just dropping by on a whim, it's purposeful" (p. 56).

Several school systems revised the principal supervisors' job descriptions to focus on instructional leadership. The draft versions of the Model Principal Supervisor Professional Standards (Council of Chief State School Officers, 2015) informed many of those decisions. These standards were deliberate in shifting the work of principal supervisors to shape and develop principals' instructional leadership capacity:

> **Standard 1.** Principal Supervisors dedicate their time to helping principals grow as instructional leaders.
>
> **Standard 2.** Principal Supervisors coach and support individual principals and engage in effective professional learning strategies to help principals grow as instructional leaders.
>
> **Standard 3.** Principal Supervisors use evidence of principals' effectiveness to determine necessary improvements in principals' practice to foster a positive educational environment that supports the diverse cultural and learning needs of students.
>
> **Standard 4.** Principal Supervisors engage principals in the formal district principal evaluation process in ways that help them grow as instructional leaders.
>
> **Standard 5.** Principal Supervisors advocate for and inform the coherence of organizational vision, policies, and strategies to support schools and student learning.

Standard 6. Principal Supervisors assist the district in ensuring the community of schools with which they engage are culturally/socially responsive and have equitable access to resources necessary for the success of each student.

Standard 7. Principal Supervisors engage in their own development and continuous improvement to help principals grow as instructional leaders.

Standard 8. Principal Supervisors lead strategic change that continuously elevates the performance of schools and sustains high-quality educational programs and opportunities across the district. (Council of Chief State School Officers, 2015, pp. 8–9)

Reducing the number of principals for each principal supervisor was another key step in Principal Supervisor Initiative districts. In some large districts, principal supervisors may be responsible for supervising dozens of principals. In many cases, a single supervisor may have responsibility for all of the district elementary principals while another supports middle and high school leaders. On average, principal supervisors in participating districts entered the initiative supervising 17 principals each. By 2017, that average declined to 12 principals each. In all cases, the goal was to give principal supervisors more time to interact with fewer principals for whom they had responsibility (Goldring et al., 2018).

The participating districts made professional learning for principal supervisors a priority. Much of the training focused on helping principal supervisors recognize quality teacher instructional practices. Such depth of understanding provided supervisors with knowledge and skills they needed to support principals in developing a similarly deep understanding of instruction. New central office structures were established to institutionalize these changes in roles and responsibilities and support succession planning (Goldring et al., 2018).

Principal learning communities provide essential peer support

While supervisors have enormous expertise and insights to offer principals, peer learning and collaboration offers an equally powerful venue for supporting principal growth. Learning Forward (2011) asserts that learning communities committed to continuous improvement, collective responsibility, and goal alignment increases educator effectiveness and results for all students. School systems that recognize the importance of professional learning communities for teachers are often the same ones that recognize similar benefits accrue when investments are made in professional learning communities for principals.

Learning communities can be used to focus principals on a shared problem of practice. Principal learning communities may identify problems of practice that emerge from issues in the school that create barriers to adult learning: What are some of the most effective ways to increase the time teachers have together to engage in a cycle of continuous improvement? In what ways can we best design learning for our mathematics team to increase its effective use of discourse in working with students? What are the best strategies for strengthening the relationship between instructional coaches and teaching teams? See Tool 8.3: Using Problems of Practice to Guide Improvement for applying this approach with principal learning communities within or among districts. In these cases, participating principals use a learning cycle to structure the processes for solving their

CHAPTER 8

problem. They analyze and discuss their findings from data in articulating the problem. They set individual school and collective community goals for their work together. They establish a learning agenda that typically includes elements of individual learning and team learning. They support each other virtually, and when possible in person, as they implement their new learning and practices. And finally they identify, collect, and analyze together formative and summative data that informs the progress they are making on solving their problems and what next steps may be required. The process is iterative. When team members resolve problems and celebrates solutions, they are energized to tackle another challenge.

Instead of working in isolation to solve their biggest challenges, principals in a community have the power of collective energy and knowledge. Principals in the learning community also share collective responsibility for the schools and students they support. Within the community, peer accountability rather than formal or administrative accountability ignites the commitment to professional learning and problem solving. Every educator and student in the schools of all principals benefit from the strengths and expertise of all the community's building leaders. New learning and better practices spread from school to school and ultimately classroom to classroom.

One of the districts in which Learning Forward helped establish principal learning communities is Clear Creek Independent School District in Texas. Describing their principal learning communities, a Clear Creek principal said, "Being in a principal community of practice has connected me more deeply with elementary and intermediate school principals. I have a larger perspective of effective leadership as a result." Instilling collective responsibility levels the playing field for students, regardless of the school they

attend, and moves a district toward greater equity. In the same district, another principal learning community focused on studying best practices of principals in higher performing districts. They were interested in the systems that supported sustained and better outcomes for students. Ultimately, they redefined their roles in relationship to leading and facilitating professional learning in their schools and with each other (Resources for Learning, 2018).

Taking action

System leaders, teachers, and parents all have valid reasons to seek and retain great school leaders. For school systems, researchers estimate a replacement cost of $75,000 per principal. Teachers and parents lose continuity, support, and valuable time in their improvement agenda when a principal leaves (Gates et al., 2019). For every 100 principals, pipeline districts saw nearly six fewer losses of principals after two years and nearly eight fewer losses after three, compared with similar schools getting new principals in other districts in their state (Gates et al., 2019). Given the evidence and exemplars offered in this chapter, the following are actions to consider in specific district contexts.

1. Formalize and assess structures to identify and invite potential leaders

From a district's perspective, decisions about who should pursue leadership shouldn't be left to chance. District leaders should take an active role in making sure those emerging leaders who have the relevant knowledge, skills, and dispositions are the ones who get tapped to move into leadership positions. While some aspiring leaders may still self-identify and seek out their own leadership growth opportunities, it's important the district have a strategy for spotting talent and actively encouraging those individuals to consider deepening their skills.

In the Wallace Principal Pipeline Initiative districts, identifying talent was a key strategy executed by each of the districts. In some cases during their school visits, district staff, including principal supervisors, were tasked with keeping their eyes open for potential talent. Brenda Turnbull and colleagues (2016) identified specific strategies employed by Principal Pipeline Initiative systems to tap talent. In New York City, for example, network and cluster leaders were specifically tasked with identifying talent when they visited schools. Charlotte-Mecklenburg participants saw their "zone executive directors as capacity builders and talent identifiers for future principals" (p. 18).

Gwinnett County and Hillsborough County leaders used their in-house principal preparation programs as the opportunity to spot and develop talent. By way of the rigorous admission processes, leaders in each district were able to spot talent early. Even though these may have been self-identified aspiring leaders, the districts had mechanisms to accelerate potential talent through the programs' admissions processes.

The building principal is also uniquely positioned to see emerging leaders early in their career. Identifying new leadership talent should be a core responsibility of effective principals. While some may see their role as helping to support succession in their own buildings, principals who assume collective responsibility for all the students in their district should also see the importance of tapping potential leadership for other positions in the system. This could range from helping identify teacher leaders to encouraging aspiring principals and district leaders to continue on the path to leadership. System leaders can take next steps by assessing formal and informal mechanisms in place to identify and encourage potential leaders. Keeping data on the success of each strategy will inform where

to concentrate efforts in the future. See Tool 8.4: Identifying the Potential to Lead for other ideas.

2. Help principals find more time to focus on instruction

Several years ago, at a leadership summit cohosted by Learning Forward and the Council of Chief State School Officers, the following question was asked of sitting principals: Is the principal's job doable? Their answers were both passionate and poignant. Although no principal said it wasn't possible to do their jobs, many of them described a set of circumstances that left the audience wondering how long they would be able to sustain their pace. They described being required to complete formal evaluations of dozens of teachers each year. They emphasized their districts' responses to their state student assessments and their roles in supporting the testing processes. They described work weeks that typically lasted 80+ hours and weekends that were all but nonexistent. It was a sobering moment and left many people in the audience concerned about all that was asked of principals.

During a meeting of The Wallace Foundation Principal Pipeline Initiative professional learning community in New York, that same question was posed to a group of superintendents from the participating districts. Several of the superintendents were quick to acknowledge their beliefs that the job of school principal is incredibly demanding and perhaps not for everyone. They affirmed the need for support in order for principals to perform effectively.

Among the many supports already discussed in this chapter, perhaps the one that principals need most is time. Principals want to allocate more time to strengthen instruction in their buildings. This means they must find ways to avoid the administrative tasks that divert their attention from this priority. There are many strategies for giving principals time (e.g. removing responsibilities, supporting them to delegate more, using central office staff differently to support building leaders). One strategy that has gained traction is the use of administration management tools such as the School Administration Manager, or SAM (http://samsconnect.com/welcome.html). The SAM project started as a Wallace-funded initiative in Louisville, Kentucky, and quickly spread to other states. The SAM program supports a shift in principals' time use from school management tasks to instructional leadership priorities. The program includes a data collection process to determine how principals spend their time and a staff member to assist principals in analyzing data and changing scheduling to prioritize instructional leadership. Researchers found that principals gained the equivalent of 27 extra days of instructional leadership time in their first year using the SAM process and more than 55 days in their third year (Turnbull et al., 2009).

3. Develop leader tracking systems

Over the course of principals' careers, they engage in numerous professional learning experiences, hold multiple positions in the district (or other districts), share a reputation for possessing certain skills or dispositions, and accumulate a history of evaluations. Often in districts, however, the data related to each of these areas exists in multiple information systems that fail to "speak" to each other. As a result, when district leaders are seeking to hire, place, or promote principals, there is no single place where they can review data about each principal candidate. Leader-tracking systems, as they have been called by Wallace Principal Pipeline Initiative districts, change that reality.

Leslie Anderson, Brenda Turnbull, and Erickson Arcaira (2017) describe leader tracking systems adopted by school systems in the Principal Pipeline Initiative to strengthen selection processes, provide on-the-job support, build a stronger bench of potential leaders, and improve pipeline components. Participating districts offer the following recommendations for districts seeking to develop their own tracking systems:

- Form a team that has a single leader and includes core information users. Make sure the team has ways to help IT staff listen to educators and vice versa. Gather ideas from other districts.
- Identify and focus on a specific purpose and an initial set of core users that the LTS will serve.
- Develop the data infrastructure through finding available data, converting it to workable formats, pulling together data that live in different systems, and validating the data — all before producing dashboards or other applications.
- Choose the right level of customization for the software, based on an assessment of existing systems.
- Begin to design the user experience. Test it. Test it again, and again. (Anderson et al., 2017, p. ii)

Jennifer Gill found that from the following types of data, district leaders will determine which will be most useful for the purposes they attach to their tracking systems:

- Educational background;
- Employment history with the district;
- Employment history outside the district;
- Ratings by teachers;
- Ratings by supervisors;
- Specialized skills (ELL, turnaround, etc.);
- Standardized test scores of students at their current school;
- Standardized test scores of students at previous schools they have led;
- Other: Mentoring and residency, completion of leadership professional development, ratings from principal screening process, teacher/student/parent

survey results of schools where principals worked, student absenteeism rate. (Gill, 2016, p. 5)

4. Support and sustain learning communities for principals and principal supervisors

Effective collaborative learning requires ongoing, planned support. Although informal networking contributes to an individual's well-being and potential effectiveness, planning and structures ensure that formal networking achieves shared goals and purposes. Principal supervisors and principals have positions that tend to isolate them from others they interact with on a day-to-day basis. A formal network with job-alike colleagues enables them to share problems and gain insights from others who understand the challenge of the position.

Learning communities are key to building collective responsibility and efficacy essential to high-performing individuals and organizations. Districts can ensure that principals and principal supervisors regularly participate in learning communities by including such participation in the job description and ensuring meeting details are posted on district calendars. Protecting time for such convenings and providing appropriate training and support increases the likelihood that the community successfully addresses shared goals and challenges and that results spread across schools.

When principals and principal supervisors participate in learning communities, they are modeling the precise practices that they expect of teachers. They are demonstrating the value they place on the time they set aside for this model of learning. In addition, when they report on their learning and outcomes, they affirm the benefits they are receiving from their investment and potentially motivate others to increase their own commitment.

Principals Influence School Systems

Principals reading this chapter to influence system leaders or principal supervisors will consider these next steps:

- Recommend this book to your principal supervisor for a book study in the school system.

- Copy and send this last chapter with a note indicating you have read the entire book and thought the recipient would find this last chapter interesting.

- Seek a meeting with a district administrator to share your key takeaways from the book and present the last chapter with your suggestions of what might be most helpful in your school system.

- If you don't have support from your school system, organize a learning community with several principals you are confident share your commitment to developing collective responsibility and continuous improvement.

- Start a journal that records all you are doing to prepare yourself for your next leadership opportunity.

CHAPTER 8

Reflections

- What are potential ideas for strengthening how our school system identifies, hires, places, supports, and appraises principals?

- What are important roles and responsibilities for principal supervisors?

- What are potential benefits for developing principal pipelines and working with principal preparation programs?

- Why is it important that principals develop their mindsets and skills as instructional leaders?

- Why is it important that school systems support individual and team learning for principals?

Conclusion

Principals who are learners seek to create conditions supportive of their own and others' learning. To succeed in that quest, they need a district's or central organization's systematic, purposeful approach to principal learning. Partner districts and organizational leaders develop ways to identify and mentor emerging leaders. They facilitate and support principal learning communities. As district and school leaders become companion learners with common goals, they shift from top-down to a collegial relationship. District leaders listen to one another and principals. They coach more often than they issue directives. They use their time with principals in high-quality professional learning rather than in briefings. Most importantly, as central office and school leaders accept that they form the district's leadership core, and thus share responsibility for the success of all learners, they move toward achieving their shared learning goals for every student and educator.

References

Anderson, L.M., Turnbull, B.J., & Arcaira, E.R. (2017). *Leader tracking systems: Turning data into information for school leadership.* Policy Studies Associates, Inc. Available at https://www.wallacefoundation.org/knowledge-center/Documents/Leader-Tracking-Systems-Turning-Data-Into-Information-for-School-Leadership.pdf

Council of Chief State School Officers. (2015). *Model Principal Supervisor Professional Standards.* Author.

Darling-Hammond, L., LaPointe, M., Meyerson, D., Orr. M. T., & Cohen, C. (2007). *Preparing school leaders for a changing world: Lessons from exemplary leadership development programs.* Stanford University, Stanford Educational Leadership Institute.

Davis, J. (2016). *Improving university principal preparation programs: Five themes from the field.* The Wallace Foundation. Available at https://www.wallacefoundation.org/knowledge-center/pages/improving-university-principal-preparation-programs.aspx

Gates, S.M., Baird, M.D., Master, B.K., & Chavez-Herrerias, E.R. (2019). *Principal pipelines: A feasible, affordable, and effective way to improve schools.* The Rand Corporation. Available at https://www.rand.org/content/dam/rand/pubs/research_reports/RR2600/RR2666/RAND_RR2666.pdf

Gill, J. (2016). *Chock full of data: How school districts are building leader tracking systems to support principal pipelines.* The Wallace Foundation. Available at https://www.wallacefoundation.org/knowledge-center/pages/chock-full-of-data-how-school-districts-are-building-leader-tracking-systems-to-support-principal-pipelines.aspx

Goldring, E.B., Clark, M.A., Rubin, M., Rogers, L.K., Grissom, J.A., Gill, B., Kautz, T., McCullough, M., Neel, M., & Burnett, A. (2020). *Changing the principal supervisor role to better support principals: Evidence from the Principal Supervisor Initiative.* Vanderbilt Peabody College, Mathematica. Available at https://www.wallacefoundation.org/knowledge-center/Documents/Changing-the-Principal-Supervisor-Role.pdf

Goldring, E. B., Grissom, J.A., Rubin, M., Rogers, L.K., Neel, M., & Clark, M.A. (2018). *A new role emerges for principal supervisors: Evidence from six districts in the Principal Supervisor Initiative.* The Wallace Foundation. Available at https://www.wallacefoundation.org/knowledge-center/Documents/A-New-Role-Emerges-for-Principal-Supervisors.pdf

Learning Forward. (2011). *Standards for Professional Learning.* Author.

Leithwood, K., Louis, K.S., Anderson, S., & Wahlstrom, K. (2004). *How leadership influences student learning.* The Wallace Foundation. Available at https://www.wallacefoundation.org/knowledge-center/pages/how-leadership-influences-student-learning.aspx

Orr, M.T., King, C., & LaPointe, M. (2010). *Districts developing leaders: Lessons on consumer actions and program approaches from eight urban districts.* Education Development Center. Available at https://www.wallacefoundation.org/knowledge-center/pages/districts-developing-leaders.aspx

Resources for Learning. (2018). *Galveston County Learning Leaders: Final report.* Unpublished external evaluation report submitted to Learning Forward and the Houston Endowment.

Turnbull, B.J., Anderson, L.M., Riley, D.L., MacFarlane, J.R., & Aladjem, D.K. (2016). *Building a stronger principalship: Volume 5.* The Wallace Foundation. Available at https://www.wallacefoundation.org/knowledge-center/pages/building-a-stronger-principalship-vol-5-the-principal-pipeline-initiative-in-action.aspx

Turnbull, B.J., Haslam, M.B., Arcaira, E.R., Riley, D.L., Sinclair, B., & Coleman, S. (2009). *Evaluation of the School Administration Manager project.* Policy Studies Associates, Inc. Available at https://www.wallacefoundation.org/knowledge-center/pages/the-school-administration-manager-project.aspx

CHAPTER 8

Tools index for Chapter 8

Tool	Title	Use
8.1	Choosing the Right Partner	This tool helps district leaders choose appropriate partners for supporting principals' preservice experiences.
8.2	Clarifying the District-University Partnership	This tool helps district leaders examine district and university partnerships to prepare school leaders.
8.3	Using Problems of Practice to Guide Improvement	This tool supports principals in bringing problems of practice to their learning communities for study and shared learning.
8.4	Identifying the Potential to Lead	This tool guides district and school leaders in recognizing and supporting potential leaders.

Authors and contributors

About the authors

Kay Psencik is a senior consultant for Learning Forward and served in Texas public schools for more than 30 years. She supports school districts and other educational organizations across the nation in efforts to transform their organizations by facilitating and coaching principals to lead high-performing schools. Psencik has supported teaching teams in developing professional learning communities that design common curriculum and instructional practices. She has coached principals in Fort Wayne Community Schools to embed professional learning into the daily lives of all staff and to raise student performance.

Psencik's other area of expertise is leadership development. She served as program designer and lead facilitator of the Principals Coalition, Twin Tiers for Learning, Inc., Corning, New York and is the designer and lead facilitator of Learning Forward's Galveston County Learning Leaders initiative. She is the co-author, with Frederick Brown and Stephanie Hirsh, of *Becoming a Learning System,* as well as the author of *The Coach's Craft.*

ABOUT THE AUTHORS

Frederick Brown is Learning Forward's chief learning officer and deputy. Prior to joining Learning Forward, Fred served as a senior program office in New York City for The Wallace Foundation where he guided the work of several major grantees, including the Southern Regional Education Board; the Institute for Learning at the University of Pittsburgh; and the states of Ohio, Iowa, Wisconsin, Oregon, Kansas, and New Jersey.

Prior to joining The Wallace Foundation, Brown was Director of the Leadership Academy and Urban Network for Chicago (LAUNCH), an organization whose mission was to identify, train, and support principals for the Chicago Public Schools. In 2005, LAUNCH was highlighted by the U.S. Department of Education as an Innovative Pathway to the Principalship.

Brown's expertise is grounded in real-world experience. He has been an elementary school teacher and principal as well as a middle school assistant principal. He also served as a founding member of the Mathematics and Equity Teams for Ohio's Project Discovery, a statewide initiative to improve mathematics and science instruction.

Over the past 15 years, Brown has been a leader in designing and facilitating cutting-edge learning experiences for school and district administrators on topics such as cultural competence, leadership, and professional learning communities.

Stephanie Hirsh is former executive director of Learning Forward. Learning Forward is an international association of more than 12,000 educators committed to increasing equity and excellence in student performance through professional learning.

Her books include two editions of *Becoming a Learning Team* with Tracy Crow (Learning Forward, 2017; 2018) and two editions of *Becoming a Learning System,* co-authored with Kay Psencik and Frederick Brown (Learning Forward, 2014; 2018); *A Playbook for Professional Learning: Putting the Standards Into Action,* co-authored with Shirley Hord (Learning Forward, 2012); and *The Learning Educator: A New Era for Professional Learning,* co-authored with Joellen Killion (NSDC, 2007). She also has written articles for *Educational Leadership, Phi Delta Kappan, The Record, The School Administrator, American School Board Journal, The High School Magazine,* and *Education Week.*

Hirsh serves on advisory boards for Learning First Alliance, Region IX (Arizona) Equity Assistance Center, Chalkboard (Oregon) Project CLASS Program; the University of Texas College of Education Advisory Council; and The Teaching Channel. She has been recognized by the Texas Staff Development Council with a Lifetime Achievement Award, and by the University of North Texas as a Distinguished Alumna.

Before joining Learning Forward, Hirsh completed 15 years of district- and school-based leadership. She has been married to Mike for more than 35 years. They have one son and a daughter who is an elementary school assistant principal.

About the contributors

Lindsay Amstutz-Martin
Principal
Fairfield Elementary
Fort Wayne
Community Schools
Fort Wayne, Indiana

Education is in Lindsay Amstutz-Martin's blood. She and her brother are fourth-generation educators descended from their great-grandmother Mable Amstutz who taught in a one-room schoolhouse during the early 1900s. Amstutz-Martin attended Indiana University, Bloomington and began her teaching career as a U.S. history and government teacher in middle and high school. Throughout her career, she also has served in various teacher leadership roles, a pathway that led her to earn an administration degree from Ball State University. After passing that milestone, she served first as an assistant principal for Fort Wayne Community Schools, and for the past eight years, as an elementary school principal.

J.R. Ankenbruck
Principal
Mabel K. Holland
Elementary School
Fort Wayne
Community Schools
Fort Wayne, Indiana

J.R. Ankenbruck has served as a teacher, assistant principal, and principal throughout his 18 years in public education. He is a strong believer in the power of shared leadership and its positive impact on equity and student success. Ankenbruck works with teacher leadership teams to develop powerful visions for school improvement so they can create long- and short-term plans for high

ABOUT THE CONTRIBUTORS

student achievement. As principal at Washington Elementary School in 2013, he and the staff realized such a vision when the school was recognized as a National Title I Distinguished School for closing the student achievement gap.

Douglas W. Anthony
Chief Consultant
Anthony Consulting Group
Bowie, Maryland

Former Associate Superintendent, Prince George's County Public Schools
Upper Marlboro, Maryland

Doug Anthony recently served as associate superintendent for talent development in Prince George's County Public Schools, one of the nation's 25 largest school districts. Throughout his career with Prince George's, he has been a teacher, principal, director of school leadership and executive director of talent management. His passion for creating leadership development programs, cultivating positive organizational cultures, and developing strategic partnerships has afforded him opportunities nationally as a speaker, presenter, and facilitator working with other school and district leaders.

Leslie Ceballos
Assistant Principal
Dr. E.T. Boon Elementary
Allen Independent
School District (ISD)
Allen, Texas

As assistant principal, Leslie Ceballos puts learning first just as she did when she was the district's technology instructional specialist and elementary science instructional specialist. Before joining Allen ISD, she worked in Richardson ISD as 3rd- and 6th-grade teacher before becoming a campus instructional coach on a Title I campus. Ceballos also is a co-designer and facilitator as part of a Learning Forward contract with the Louisiana Department of Education that engages teacher leaders across the state in a mentor cycle to become effective mentors. She has drawn on her experience as a Title I instructional coach as a presenter for Learning Forward annual conferences and a contributor to the Learning Forward publication *Becoming a Learning Team.*

Leilani Esmond
Director
Department of
Staff Development
Gwinnett County
Public Schools
Gwinnett County, Georgia

Leilani Esmond, director of the staff development department for Gwinnett County Public Schools is also the current president of Learning Forward Georgia. Esmond's work is influenced by her experience as an elementary school teacher, local school and district instructional coach, and high school administrator. Facilitating the positive effects of high-quality educator professional learning on student achievement and development fuels her passion and love for education.

ABOUT THE CONTRIBUTORS

Rachel Harris
Principal
Santa Fe High School
Santa Fe Independent
School District (ISD)
Santa Fe, Texas

Rachel Harris served the Santa Fe ISD community for 19 years as a teacher, assistant principal, and principal of Santa Fe Junior High. She then became director of learning and is currently principal of Santa Fe High School. Harris guides teachers through the process of continuous improvement by utilizing learning designs in professional learning communities. She mentors and cultivates leadership within her building. Part of that work entails helping teacher leaders and assistant principals navigate professional learning communities so they focus on learning and continuous improvement of their practice.

Carrie Kennedy
Principal
Fred H. Croninger
Elementary School
Fort Wayne
Community Schools
Fort Wayne, Indiana

During her 23-year career Carrie Kennedy has educated students ranging from youngsters to adults. Her curiosity is what propels her to be a learning principal. And for the past decade she has applied that curiosity and focus on learning as the principal of one of Fort Wayne Community Schools' Four-Star Schools, which rank in the top 25% in achievement for the state. Her school won that designation for the past six years of her leadership. She has led, coached, and mentored teachers and administrative interns, many of whom she continues to motivate so they realize their professional potential. Kennedy offers her experience at the district level by serving on district committees convened to develop professional growth through new learning or focused, precise feedback.

Destini Martin
Principal
William F. Barnett
Elementary
Santa Fe Independent
School District (ISD)
Santa Fe, Texas

Destini Martin has been working with Learning Forward on school improvement and communities of practice for the past five years through as a participant in the Galveston County Learning Leaders initiative funded by the Houston Endowment. She also has presented at the Annual Learning Forward Conference on shifting educator practice. For the last 10 years Martin has been an administrator in Santa Fe ISD and served as head principal during half that time. At the start of the 2019–20 school year, she stepped into a different role: Senior principal. In that new role she will mentor and coach new principals.

Stephanie Montez
Principal
Adams Elementary
Mesa Public Schools
Mesa, Arizona

Stephanie Montez has been an elementary school teacher, assistant principal, an academic coach, and elementary school principal throughout her education career. For the last 10 years, she has been an elementary school principal and instructional leader at two different schools. During her tenure at both schools, they were transformed into model schools that were visited regularly by other school and district administrators from around the state. Before becoming a principal, Montez was an assistant principal and an academic coach

ABOUT THE CONTRIBUTORS

helping teachers to improve their practice. She continues to help school staffs strengthen instructional practice as a staff developer for AVID. In that role Montez travels the country helping schools and districts learn how to ensure that their students are college- and career ready.

Azra Redzic
Elementary
Humanities Supervisor
Bristol Public Schools

Former Principal
Maria Sanchez
Elementary School
Bristol, Connecticut

Azra Redzic began her education career in Hartford, Connecticut Public Schools 14 years ago. Starting as a classroom teacher, she became an intervention specialist and culminated her final four years as principal of Maria Sanchez Elementary School. Currently, she is the elementary humanities supervisor for Bristol Public Schools. In that capacity she oversees curriculum development and instruction for English language arts and social studies for preschool through 5th grade. Redzic is responsible for providing teachers and administrators with professional learning related to curriculum, instruction, assessment, culture and climate, and district priorities. As co-chair for the School Readiness Council, she ensures that high-quality education begins with early learners. Her current focus is ensuring a rigorous curriculum and school culture dedicated to building academic excellence, relationships, and social and emotional learning.

Christel Swinehart-Arbogast
Principal
Emerson Elementary
Mesa Public Schools
Mesa, Arizona

In her 23-year career, Christel Swinehart-Arbogast has served as a teacher, instructional coach, Title I school improvement specialist, and principal. While gaining rich experience in teaching and learning, she has developed her passion for providing or engaging in high-quality professional learning for her colleagues, staff members, and herself. Recognizing her commitment to professional learning, the Arizona Department of Education tapped Swinehart-Arbogast to participate in Learning Forward's Leadership Academy and Learning Leaders for Learning Schools initiative funded by the Houston Endowment. She also partners with Arizona State University (ASU) in the Project Enhancement Team conducted through ASU's Mary Lou Fulton Teachers College.